"Woodcarvers' Favorite P

Book Three

Nature in Wood

Great Patterns for Carving
21 Birds and 8 Wild Animals

edited by David Hunt

patterns by George Lehman

Fox Chapel Publishing

Publishers of Fine Books

Box 7948A Lancaster PA 17604

copyright 1991 Fox Chapel Publishing Co. Inc.
all rights reserved
Library of Congress # 91-75524
ISBN # 1-56523-006-X

"Nature in Wood" is Book Three in the Woodcarvers Favorite Patterns series
Other volumes available:
Book One: Carving 20 Realistic Game and Song Birds
Book Two   Realism in Wood - 22 Projects
Book Three   Nature in Wood - 29 Great Projects
Book Four   Carving Wildlife in Wood -20 Exciting Projects
See appendix section in the back of this volume for complete details.

WOODCARVERS' FAVORITE PATTERNS and the logo/design with a fox are trademarks of
Fox Chapel Publishing

The carving on the cover of this book was carved by Ed Hearn, Hendersonville, Tennessee
photograph copyright by Ed Hearn , used by permission
Ed can be reached where he works :
PHILLIPS PRINTING CO. INC.
949 Woodland St.
Nashville , Tennessee   37206
(615) - 227 - 5466

Manufactured in the United States of America

Nature In Wood

TABLE OF CONTENTS

Subject   *Page*

BIRD PROJECTS

Continued next page - ANIMAL PROJECTS & CARICATURES

Table of Contents - continued

Carving friends

I wish to remind you that I'm an artist and a woodcarver like yourself. If you find any grammatical errors — please overlook them. I don't profess to be a writer, I'm only trying to explain my way of carving these patterns.

In this book I have put in birds from around the United States and Canada, plus many field sketches that could be used as patterns by some of you creative carvers. In addition to the twenty birds, I have included animal patterns that I felt you would enjoy, plus a pattern of my two favorite people, Belle and Cactus Pete.

I hope you enjoy carving all of these as much as I have.

Keep carving,

your friend

GEORGE
Lehman

REDSTART

1

INTRODUCTION

My lovely wife and I are fortunate to live in such a beautiful state as Minnesota where wildlife abounds. We love the outdoors and all of God's wonderful family.

It is my opinion that you must know your subject, before you can create a likeness. You cannot hurry a fine carving — take time to do it right. The extra time spent will be rewarded when the carving is completed. Each and every carving should be a little better than the last one — if not, you are not observing or listening — be gracious enough to accept constructive critizism. We all learn from others.

Patience and creative thinking is the secret to master carving — join a club, you can learn from others and you will enjoy sharing your knowledge with others.

Carve to please yourself.

GEORGE
Lehman

"Willie" at the helm
in Winnipeg . . .

WREN

2

THE GAMBEL QUAIL

The Gambel Quail a ground nesting, prolific bird, laying from 12 to 15 eggs per clutch. The young can usually fly short distances at the age of a week or so. Most Quail remain in family groups, sometimes as many as 100 in a covey.

The male, or rooster must be cut from 2 pieces of wood, because of the grain needed for strength in the bill. The hen pattern is such that it can be cut from one piece of wood.

We will carve the male bird first, both have the same basic feathers so these instructions can be used for both birds. Carve the head first (note the crest feather is an insert). When the head is carved and textured to your satisfaction, insert the eyes and form the eye lids. (see section on inserting eyes)

Dowel and glue the head to the rough cut body. You may want to turn the head a little. When this is dry, carve the body to shape and sand very carefully. Draw the top feathers. Carve and burn the feather texture. Draw the tail feathers, carve and burn these on both sides. Draw the side feathers, carve these. The primary feathers are to be carved, not inserted, so now is the time to cut these to the proper shape. When you burn these feathers, **both** sides must be textured because the inside will show if carved right. Draw the belly feathers, these are soft feathers and must be stoned rathen than carved. Stone or bur hills and valleys, sand, redraw and cut feather splits with a small flat stone, cut the feather texture (see illustration in Blue Jay section).

Repeat these instructions for carving the hen. When both birds are complete, arrange them on the mount you have selected. The leg wires should be heavy enough to support these birds. Position the birds and drill holes in the mount to accomodate the leg rods. Drill holes into the bird and glue these rods. Finish the legs and feet as shown on pattern.

Perhaps you'll want to carve a cactus or some desert type of plant.

These are beautiful when painted, and will be a real conversation piece in your collection. Have fun and take your time. Keep carving.

KINGFISHER

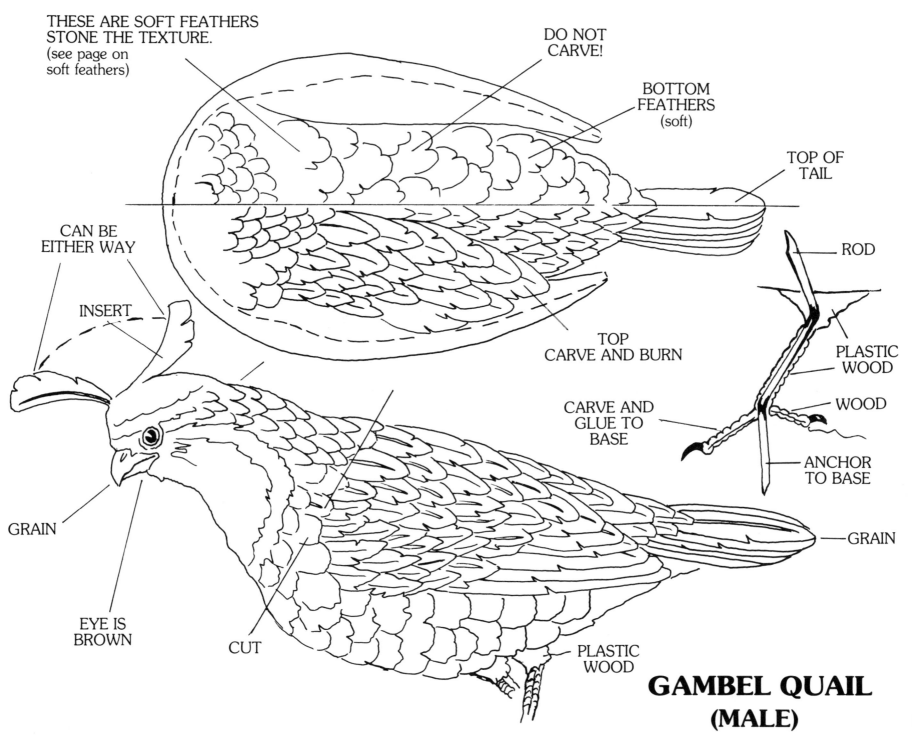

THESE ARE SOFT FEATHERS
STONE THE TEXTURE.
(see page on
soft feathers)

DO NOT
CARVE!

BOTTOM
FEATHERS
(soft)

TOP OF
TAIL

ROD

PLASTIC
WOOD

WOOD

CAN BE
EITHER WAY

INSERT

TOP
CARVE AND BURN

CARVE AND
GLUE TO
BASE

ANCHOR
TO BASE

GRAIN

GRAIN

EYE IS
BROWN

CUT

PLASTIC
WOOD

**GAMBEL QUAIL
(MALE)**

5

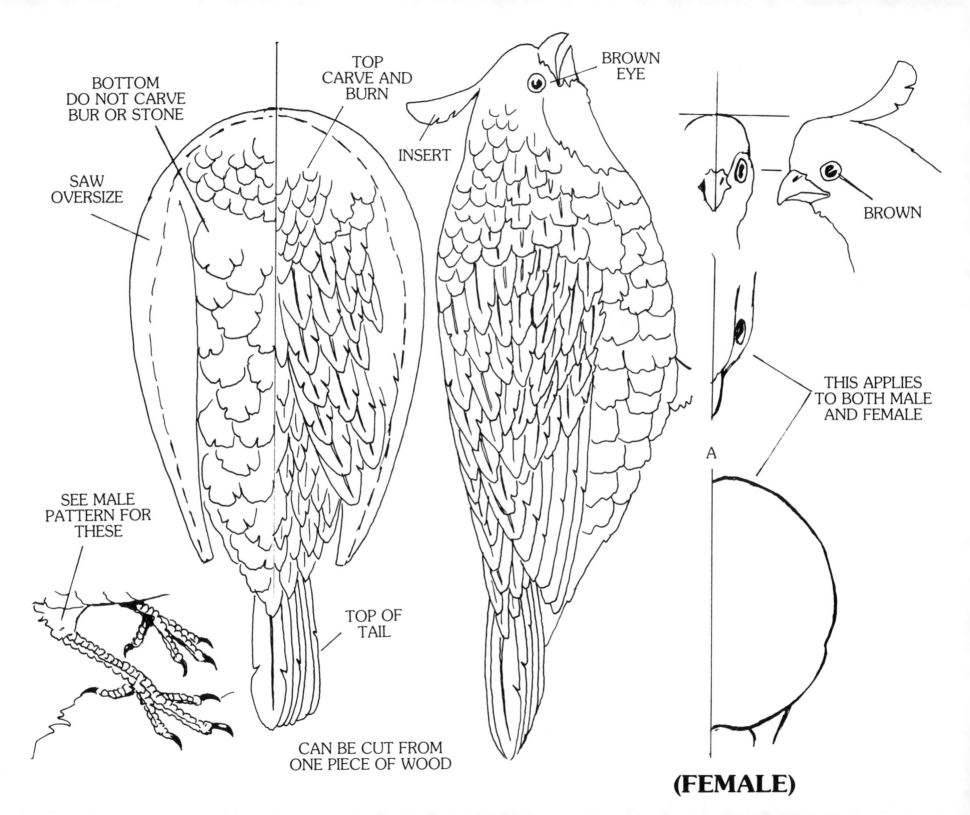

BOTTOM
DO NOT CARVE
BUR OR STONE

SAW
OVERSIZE

TOP
CARVE AND
BURN

INSERT

BROWN
EYE

BROWN

THIS APPLIES
TO BOTH MALE
AND FEMALE

SEE MALE
PATTERN FOR
THESE

TOP OF
TAIL

A

CAN BE CUT FROM
ONE PIECE OF WOOD

6

(FEMALE)

THE CLIFF SWALLOW

The Cliff Swallow is usually found near water in open country cliffs, farmlands with bridges or buildings for nesting. These are the swallows that return to capistrano each year around March 19th.

This carving must be made in two pieces because of the grain of the wood. You'll need the strength of the grain for the bill. Perhaps you will want to turn the head a little, it always adds to the realism of the bird. Carve the head first, insert the eyes and texture the head. Dowel and glue the head to the rough body. Carve the body to shape and sand very carefully. If you have a definite line showning at the glue joint, V out an area and fill with plastic wood. Let this dry and then sand. Draw the back feathers, carve and burn (note the tail coverts) they must fit into the undercut you make on the last row of feathers. Draw the side feathers, carve and burn again. Undercut the secondaries so the primary inserts will fit in. Draw the belly feathers, these as before are very soft feathers, and must be burred or stoned. Do not carve feather stop cuts. Burn these feathers. cut any feather splits before you burn the texture.

Create something different for the mount, it's always fun to try new ideas. Have fun, keep carving.

GEORGE
Lehman

BACKGROUND IS IMPORTANT . . .

Some carvers design the base and background material first, then carve a bird to fit the piece. This may work real well for many, however, I prefer to plan both my background and bird together. I deside on the bird I will carve and then I draw the pattern. If I have a suitable piece of driftwood for this bird I'll sketch up the whole idea. If it looks good on paper, chances are it will come out pretty well. While carving the bird I keep in mind which way it will be looking, what it will be doing, and how it will look to the viewer.

The whole piece to me must fit together like a puzzle. Each section must compliment the next. Remember, do not overwork your base — if there is any one thing that can ruin an otherwise fine carving, it would be an overworked background. The base and background should compliment your carving, but not over shadow it.

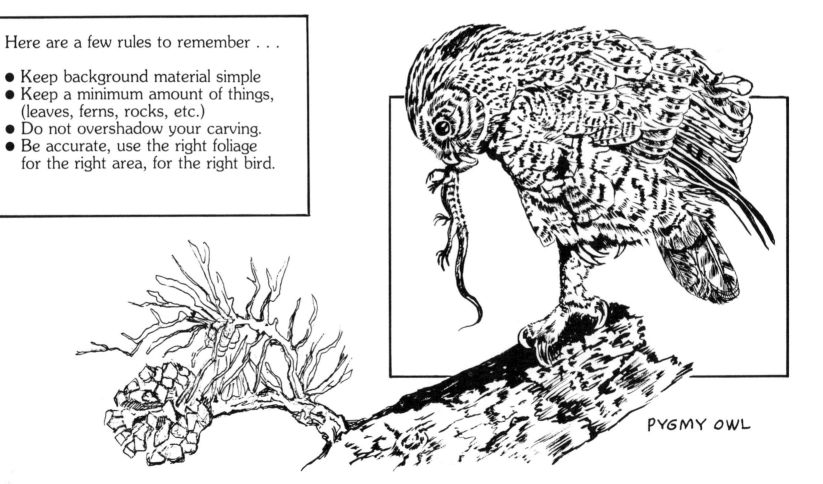

Here are a few rules to remember . . .

- Keep background material simple
- Keep a minimum amount of things, (leaves, ferns, rocks, etc.)
- Do not overshadow your carving.
- Be accurate, use the right foliage for the right area, for the right bird.

PYGMY OWL

THE CLIFF SWALLOW

APPROX 5" to 6"

INSERTS

VERY SOFT
FEATHERS

BOTTOM
OF TAIL

LEG HOLE

A

A

INSERTS

CURVE TAIL

TOP OF TAIL

SEE SIDE
PATTERN

NOTE VERY
SMALL FEATHERS
HERE

EYES
ARE BROWN

BENT 1/16" ROD

ANCHOR TO
BIRD

PLASTIC
WOOD

WOOD OR
LEAD

ANCHOR TO
BASE

TAIL
SLOT

INSERTS

INSERTS

GRAIN

SEAL CRACK
WITH PLASTIC WOOD

BEND AROUND
MOUNT

INSERT

UNDER CUT
TO ACCEPT
INSERT

BOB-O-LINK

This colorful beauty can be found in moist open fields, meadows, farmlands and marshes. They migrate each fall to South America.

Unless you wish to turn the head of this bird, you need not carve the head separate. However, I would insert the tail, the tail coverts and the primaries.

Carve the head first. You will note the small feathers on the head, do these with your iron, **do not carve.** Draw the back feathers, carve, sand and burn (note last row are inserts). Draw the side feathers, undercut the secondaries to accomodate the primary inserts. Draw in the belly feathers, these must appear very soft, **do not carve stops**. Bur or stone and burn in texture. Mount tail and tail coverts. Mount primaries.

Select a mount for this beautiful bird. Drill the holes for his feet. Insert the leg wires into the body, build up leg shank with plastic wood. Paint the bird before you mount it, its easier. Carve some fake leaves and acorns for your background. Mount the bird when it's dry. Sit back and admire another of your masterpieces.

Fun isn't it? Keep carving.

GEORGE
Lehman

Let's make a leaf . . .

Many have asked how I make my foliage for my birds — One way would be carving — It's a great way, but the leaves are not too durable, and the frustration of carving something that thin sometimes isn't worth it. You could use thin shim stock, copper or brass however that also has its draw backs. Let's consider paper — To illustrate we'll make one oak leaf.

The paper must be of a fairly hard finish, and at least a cover weight. I found that a plain brown office folder would make a beautiful leaf. In a step by step process let's begin —

SPARROWS ON A
BRISK FALL DAY...

1. Make a drawing of the leaf you need for your carving (in this case an oak leaf).

2. Be sure the leaf is of the proper size for your carving — for instance, if you are making an oak leaf for the Blue Jay, make the leaf almost as large as the Jay.

3. Trace your drawing on the paper you have selected.

4. Tape several sheets together, and with a sharp exacto cut out the leaf.

5. You now have three or four blanks to work with. Drop them in a dish of water.

6. When soaked, remove one and lay in on a piece of blotter.

7. With a blunt tool, put in the main lines of leaf, be carefull not to press too hard so you rupture the paper surface. Let this dry some more.

8. When the leaf is almost dry, put in the finer lines from the main stem — let the leaf dry completely.

9. Glue a wood stem on the leaf.

10. Spray the leaf with a WORKABLE Krylon fixative. Let this dry and spray several times.

11. Paint the leaf, and spray one more time with the fixative.

12. You now have a durable leaf that you can glue to your mount. Try to attach leaves in a position where they will be in no danger of being bumped.

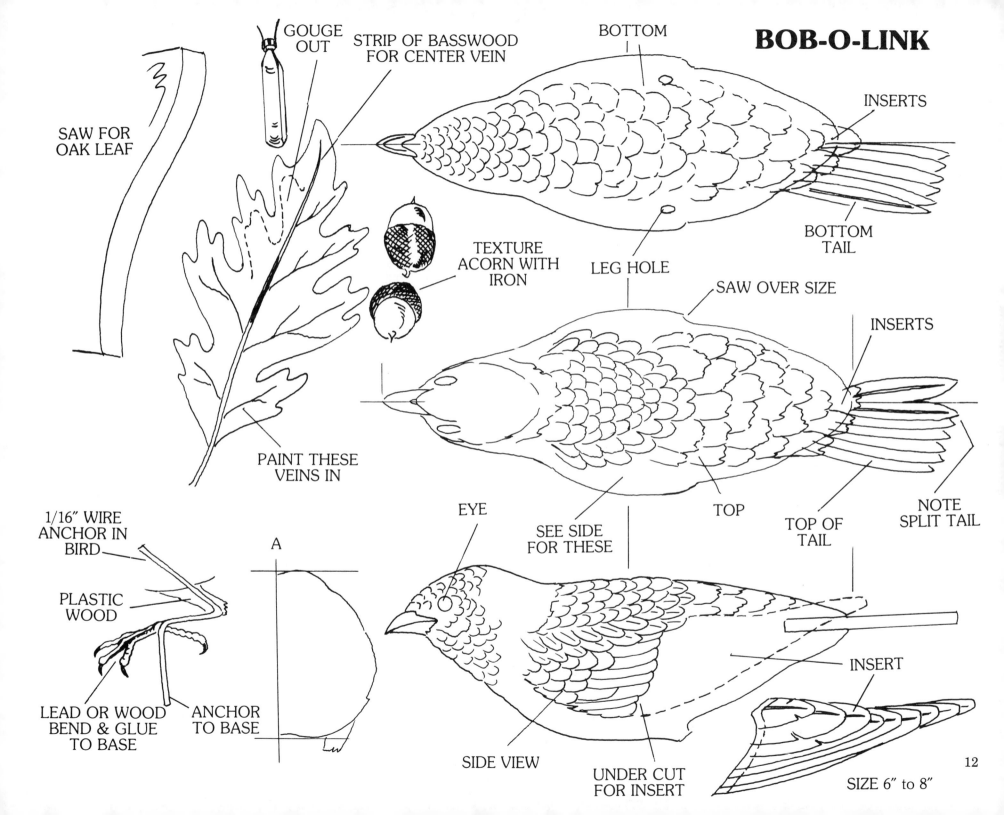

BOB-O-LINK

GOUGE OUT

STRIP OF BASSWOOD FOR CENTER VEIN

BOTTOM

INSERTS

SAW FOR OAK LEAF

TEXTURE ACORN WITH IRON

LEG HOLE

BOTTOM TAIL

SAW OVER SIZE

INSERTS

PAINT THESE VEINS IN

SEE SIDE FOR THESE

TOP

TOP OF TAIL

NOTE SPLIT TAIL

1/16" WIRE ANCHOR IN BIRD

A

EYE

PLASTIC WOOD

LEAD OR WOOD BEND & GLUE TO BASE

ANCHOR TO BASE

INSERT

SIDE VIEW

UNDER CUT FOR INSERT

SIZE 6" to 8"

12

CAPE MAY WARBLER

This beautiful little Cape May Warbler migrates with the rest of the many kinds of warblers, to the deep south every year. He has been seen in the West Indies and South America. He returns to the northern regions about May.

This beauty can be carved from one piece of wood, however I think the primaries should be inserted. It may be easier when you burn the feathers.

Saw the body slightly oversized, complete the head first, drill the holes for the eyes and set them with plastic wood. Use a small brush and wood thinner to form the eyelids. When dry, texture the head with your burning tool.

Rough in the body and sand. Draw the top pattern, carve and burn. Draw the side patterns and carve, if you insert the primaries you must undercut the secondaries to accept these. Carve the tail and burn the completed sides and tail.

Draw in the soft feathers on the belly, bur these, do not carve. When you have roughed these, carve some splits and sand. Texture these with a stone or your burning tool. Make the primary inserts, texture them on both sides and insert them.

Select a good piece of driftwood for your mount. Arrange some type of leaf or foliage arrangement, do not over do! Drill holes in your bird for leg wires, line them up on the mount and drill into the mount. Glue the bird to the mount. When dry carve the toes from wood or lead. Glue them in place as shown on pattern — patch any defects you have with plastic wood.

Build the leg shank with plastic wood and when dry texture with a low heat iron (see pattern).

You now have a fine warbler ready to paint. The brilliant colors of this beauty will really make a fine show piece.

Have fun and keep carving.

ROSE FINCH..

The Cheetah . . .
Speed demon of
the African Plains

CAPE MAY WARBLER

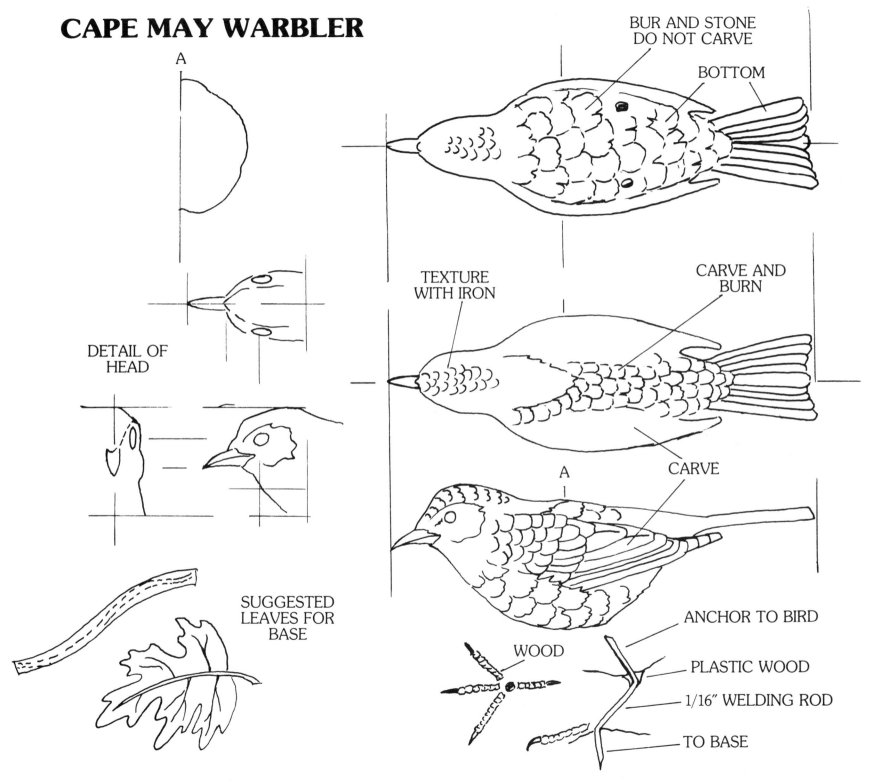

A

BUR AND STONE
DO NOT CARVE

BOTTOM

DETAIL OF
HEAD

TEXTURE
WITH IRON

CARVE AND
BURN

A

CARVE

SUGGESTED
LEAVES FOR
BASE

WOOD

ANCHOR TO BIRD

PLASTIC WOOD

1/16" WELDING ROD

TO BASE

15

BLUE JAY

Noted for his noisey, sometimes mean disposition, the Blue Jay is one of our more colorful birds. His active, cockey manners makes him a delight to carve. His approximate size is from 11″ to 12½″. If you make him full size, as the pattern shows, you can cut his body from 2½″ x 2½″ x 4½″ Basswood. The head and tail are separate. The head should be carved with the grain of the wood running the same direction as the bill (see pattern). Carve the head first, leave enough wood at the base of the neck to insure plenty of carving wood when you join the head to the body. When carving the bill, notice how the bill is straight back from tip to the head. Do not get the bill too heavy. The hood of the Jay is textured with a small bur or stone and finished with your burning iron. Very carefully spot the eye holes and drill them slightly oversized, set them in plastic wood, allowing some

of the plastic to overlap the hole. With a small brush, some solvent, and care, paint in the eyelids. When you are finished with the head, dowel and glue it to the roughed in body, now is the time to turn the head for a little action in the carving. When dry, rough carve the body, sand very carefully, transfer the top feathers. Be sure you use a center line completely around the bird. Notice the yoke on the top of the bird, these feathers should be very soft appearing, do not carve these! Simply bur or stone these feathers and texture them with your iron. Trace the rest of the top feathers. Carve them to the point where the tail inserts begin. If the carving is too deep, sand each feather to give them a rounded appearance, burn them for texture as shown.

16

Trace the two sides, carve these feathers and again burn the feather texture. Allow an undercut where the primaries insert (see pattern). Please note the top yoke and the lower side feathers overlap the wing pattern (see pattern).

Draw the belly feathers, **do not** carve these, rough them with a small bur or stone and detail the feathers with your iron. These should appear very soft. Carve the tail and the two primary inserts. Insert the tail first and insert the coverts. Insert the two wing primaries.

You are now ready to mount your Blue Jay. Select a piece of drift wood that will go well with your carving, figure out the way you would like to place the legs and feet and proceed to put on the leg wires (as shown). There are several ways of making the feet, each are shown in detail on the back of the Grosbeak page.

Keep carving, have fun.

"SOFT FEATHERS"

1. Pencil the outline of the "soft" feathers
2. With a stone or small bur, create "soft" feathers as "hills and valleys."
3. Sand carefully, redraw the feathers — with a sharp pointed knife cut the feather splits.
4. With a small flat stone texture each feather as shown. Clean out the texture with small wire brush or tooth brush.

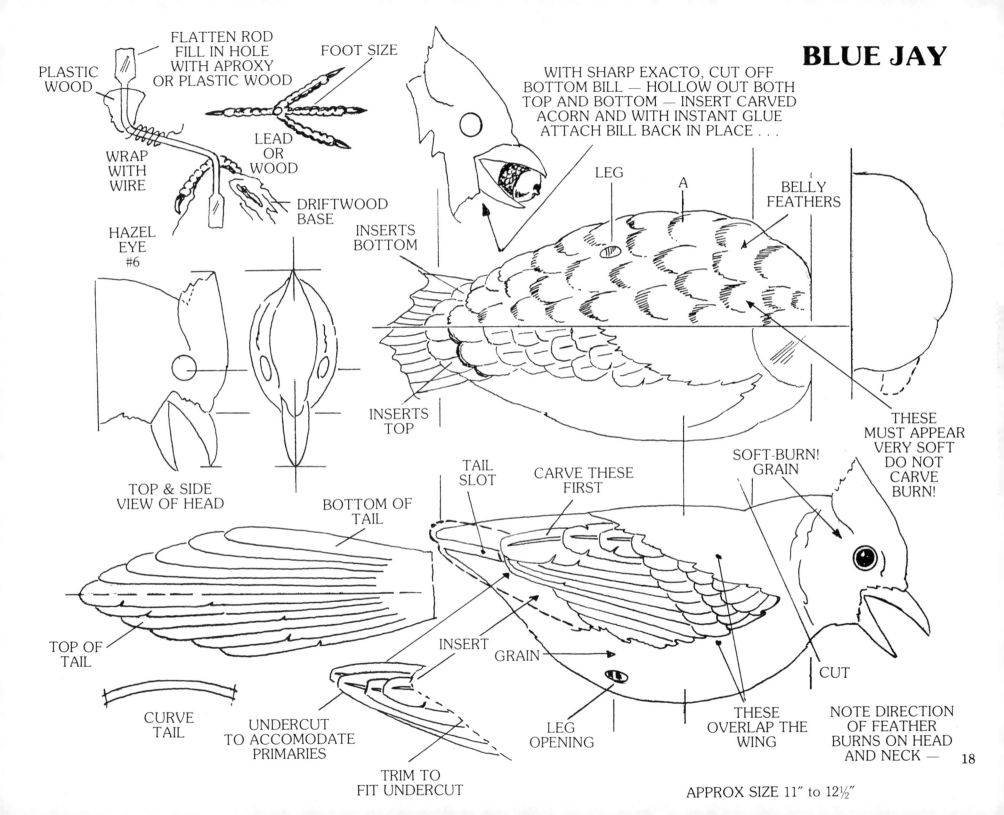

BLUE JAY

PLASTIC WOOD

FLATTEN ROD FILL IN HOLE WITH APROXY OR PLASTIC WOOD

FOOT SIZE

WITH SHARP EXACTO, CUT OFF BOTTOM BILL — HOLLOW OUT BOTH TOP AND BOTTOM — INSERT CARVED ACORN AND WITH INSTANT GLUE ATTACH BILL BACK IN PLACE . . .

WRAP WITH WIRE

LEAD OR WOOD

HAZEL EYE #6

DRIFTWOOD BASE

INSERTS BOTTOM

LEG

A

BELLY FEATHERS

INSERTS TOP

TOP & SIDE VIEW OF HEAD

BOTTOM OF TAIL

THESE MUST APPEAR VERY SOFT DO NOT CARVE BURN!

TAIL SLOT

CARVE THESE FIRST

SOFT-BURN! GRAIN

TOP OF TAIL

INSERT

GRAIN

CUT

CURVE TAIL

UNDERCUT TO ACCOMODATE PRIMARIES

LEG OPENING

THESE OVERLAP THE WING

NOTE DIRECTION OF FEATHER BURNS ON HEAD AND NECK —

TRIM TO FIT UNDERCUT

APPROX SIZE 11" to 12½"

18

CACTUS WREN

A large sized wren, 7 to 8 inches in length, nests in thorny shrub or cactus. They range from California, Nevada, Utah and Texas to Central America.

This wren can be carved with the head and body as one piece, however I would insert the tail. Carve the head first, notice how long and sharp the bill appears. Texture the head with your burning iron, use very short strokes to simulate small, fine feathers. The eye should be inserted and the eyelid made before you start carving the feathers on the body. When you have completed the head, carve and sand the body to shape. Draw in the top pattern and carve and burn these feathers. Draw the side patterns. Pay attention to the pattern (the belly feathers overlap the side feathers). When you have cut the primaries as shown draw this pattern and carve the side feathers, burn the texture. Carve and texture the tail on both sides. Insert the tail and the tail coverts. When these are complete, both top and bottom, draw in the belly feathers, these are soft feathers **do not carve.** Bur in the feathers forming hills and valleys, sand very carefully and stone the feather texture as shown on the Blue Jay page.

You now have a beautiful Cactus Wren that must be set into a proper setting of the desert. Use your creative talents. The efforts you put into the mounting will either make or break a fine carving. The feet and legs are as shown on the pattern, either wood or lead, with plastic wood to cover any imperfections.

Have patience and take your time, each and every carving will be better. We all learn with every carving.
Have fun!

Reed Bunting..

When mounting a bird first pick an interesting piece of drift wood or root that will accomodate your carving. This should not be so large as to take away from your art. It should be strong enough to support the bird. I usually mount the driftwood to a base for added support. If the bird is standing, you have no problem. Drill two holes and adjust the anchor wires as you want. If the bird is flying, find enough room back, or side of bird to drill two holes through the driftwood into the carving. In one hole counter sink a small screw. In the other place a pin to prevent the carving from turning on the screw. Glue the carving, the screw and pin.

The background or decorations on each piece should be secured enough to prevent breaking when the carving is cleaned or handled. For example, if you carve a cat tail, make the stem of the cat tail of wire, flexible enough to withstand a few bumps without bending. A leaf such as oak, maple or willow should be secured in at least (2) two places with glue.

I personally like to keep the mount (driftwood) as free from other objects as possible, so the carving will get the most attention.

To clean up an average piece of driftwood into something very exotic, use a small bur on your power tool and go over the whole piece, putting in a weather beaten texture. You'll be delighted how beautifully a rather dull piece will suddenly become very interesting.

The way you present your carving will enhance it. It would be a shame to put a truly fine carving on a rather mediocre mounting. So be creative and as you carve, plan the type of setting you would like to see your bird in.

CACTUS WREN

6" to 8½"

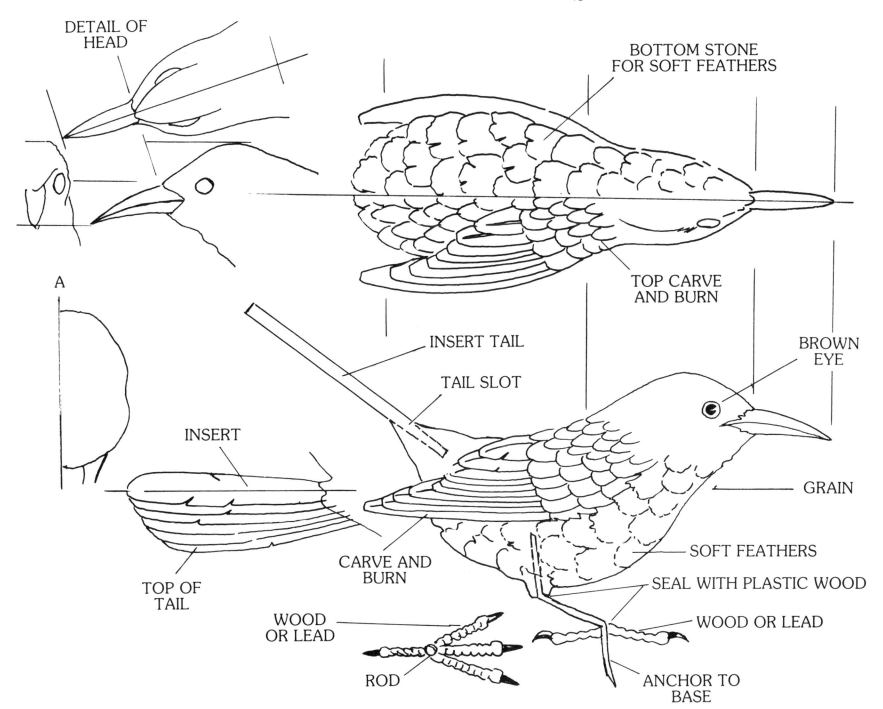

DETAIL OF HEAD

BOTTOM STONE FOR SOFT FEATHERS

TOP CARVE AND BURN

A

INSERT TAIL

TAIL SLOT

BROWN EYE

INSERT

GRAIN

SOFT FEATHERS

TOP OF TAIL

CARVE AND BURN

SEAL WITH PLASTIC WOOD

WOOD OR LEAD

WOOD OR LEAD

ROD

ANCHOR TO BASE

21

EVENING GROSBEAK

The Evening Grosbeak is an irregular migrant. Usually building it's nest in Canada and migrating to the great lakes in winter, however he has been known to go as far south as Kentucky and as far west as California. He is about 8" long, with a large conical bill. This carving can be from a 2¼" x 2¼" x 4" piece of basswood **if** you insert the tail, and make the head as a separate piece. I would recommend this to insure proper grain in the beak. Carve the head first, if this comes out well the rest of the bird comes easy. You will note on the pattern how the bottom beak is cut off, hollowed out, berry inserted and reglued with out seeing the joint. When you are satisfied with the head, dowel and glue it to the body blank. Rough in body, sand very carefully and transfer the top pattern. The yoke feathers are very soft, do **not** carve these, use a small bur or stone to indicate these. Carve the balance of the top feathers, burn these and the head. Draw the side feathers, carve, sand and burn. Under cut the last row to accept the primary inserts. Carve the tail, glue and insert the tail coverts. The belly feathers are also burred or stoned to appear very soft — texture with iron.

Select a good piece of driftwood to display this beauty —I used the small rod, wood, and plastic wood method of making my legs and feet (see page on feet).

Remember, use the right foliage and berries for the local of the Grosbeak.

Have fun and Keep Carving!

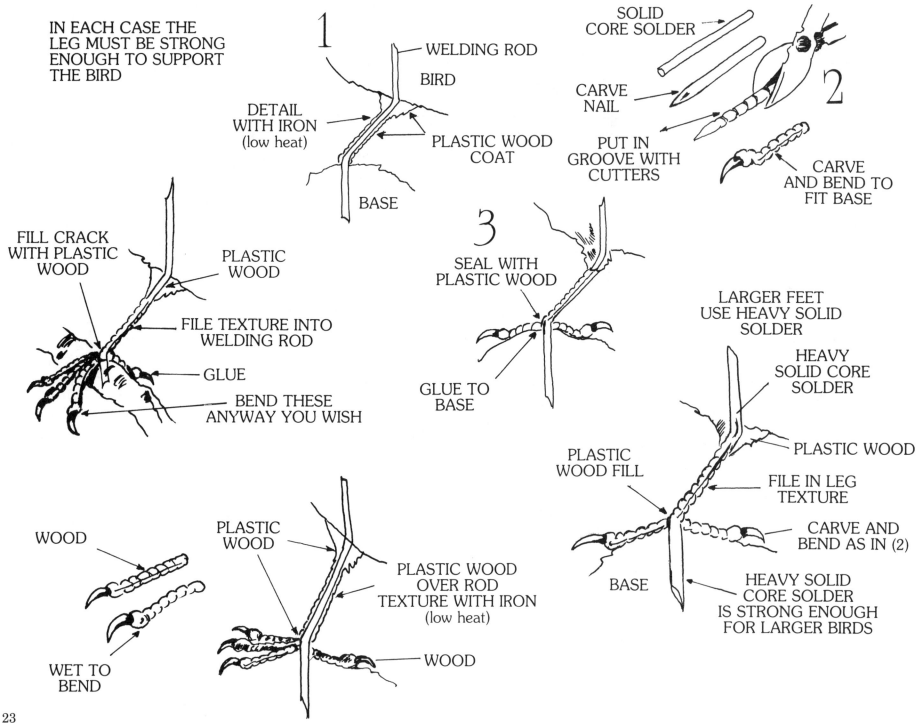

IN EACH CASE THE LEG MUST BE STRONG ENOUGH TO SUPPORT THE BIRD

1
WELDING ROD
BIRD
DETAIL WITH IRON (low heat)
PLASTIC WOOD COAT
BASE

2
SOLID CORE SOLDER
CARVE NAIL
PUT IN GROOVE WITH CUTTERS
CARVE AND BEND TO FIT BASE

FILL CRACK WITH PLASTIC WOOD
PLASTIC WOOD
FILE TEXTURE INTO WELDING ROD
GLUE
BEND THESE ANYWAY YOU WISH

3
SEAL WITH PLASTIC WOOD
GLUE TO BASE

LARGER FEET USE HEAVY SOLID SOLDER
HEAVY SOLID CORE SOLDER
PLASTIC WOOD
FILE IN LEG TEXTURE
PLASTIC WOOD FILL
CARVE AND BEND AS IN (2)
BASE
HEAVY SOLID CORE SOLDER IS STRONG ENOUGH FOR LARGER BIRDS

WOOD
WET TO BEND
PLASTIC WOOD
PLASTIC WOOD OVER ROD TEXTURE WITH IRON (low heat)
WOOD

23

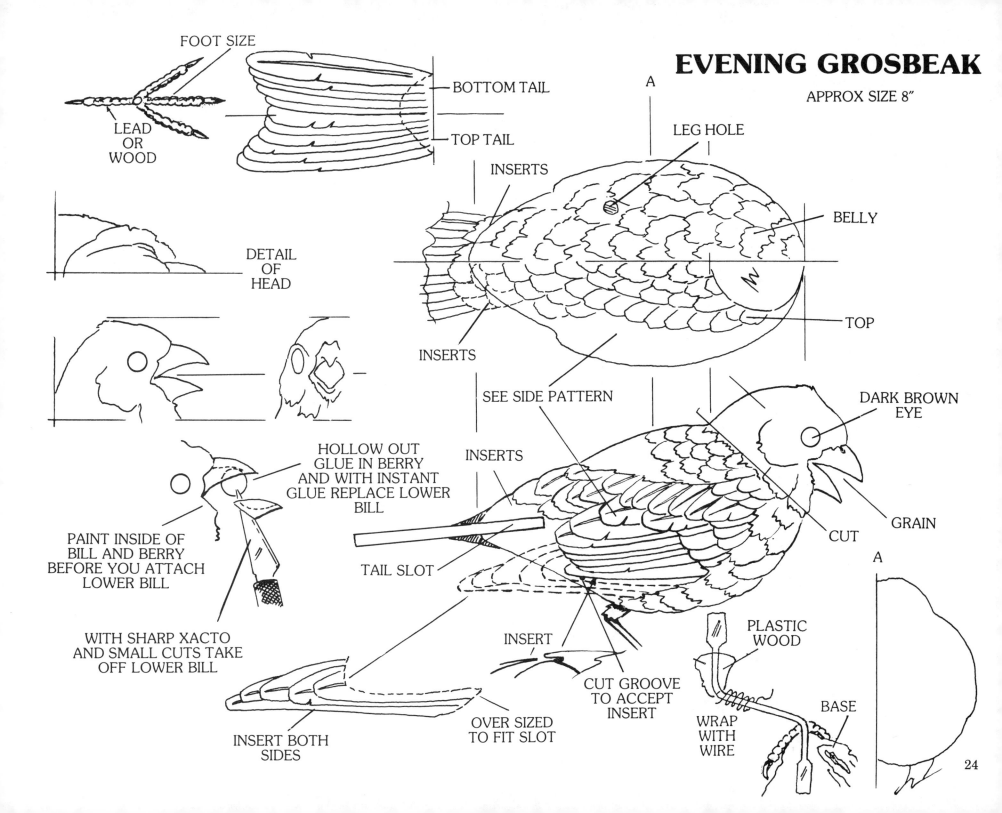

EVENING GROSBEAK

APPROX SIZE 8"

FOOT SIZE

LEAD OR WOOD

BOTTOM TAIL

TOP TAIL

A

LEG HOLE

INSERTS

BELLY

DETAIL OF HEAD

INSERTS

TOP

SEE SIDE PATTERN

DARK BROWN EYE

HOLLOW OUT GLUE IN BERRY AND WITH INSTANT GLUE REPLACE LOWER BILL

INSERTS

PAINT INSIDE OF BILL AND BERRY BEFORE YOU ATTACH LOWER BILL

CUT

GRAIN

A

TAIL SLOT

WITH SHARP XACTO AND SMALL CUTS TAKE OFF LOWER BILL

PLASTIC WOOD

INSERT

CUT GROOVE TO ACCEPT INSERT

BASE

INSERT BOTH SIDES

OVER SIZED TO FIT SLOT

WRAP WITH WIRE

24

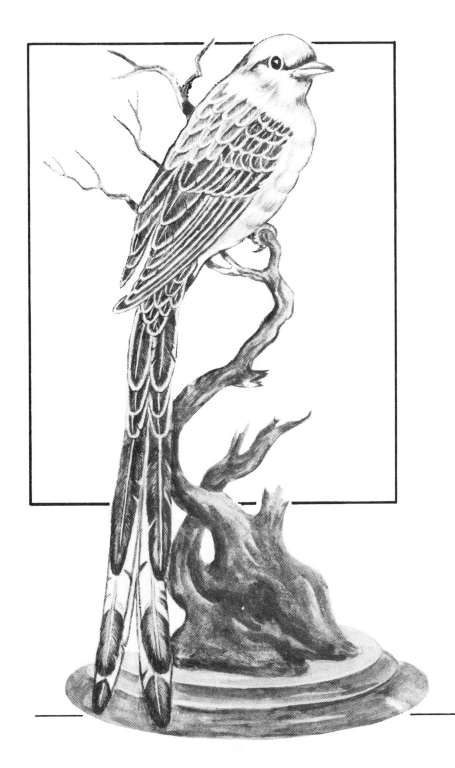

SCISSOR-TAILED FLYCATCHER

The Scissor-Tailed Flycatcher lives in open bushy areas with scattered trees, poles, high wires or other high perches. A real south western beauty.

As always, carve the head first! In this case it must be separate because of the grains. When the head is carved to your satisfaction, insert the eyes and burn the texture with very short fine lines. Mount the head to the rough sawn body. Carve the body and sand very carefully. Draw in the top feathers (note the tail inserts) they must fit into the last row carved. Draw the side feathers, carve to where the primaries insert, under cut the secondaries to accomodate these. Burn these. Draw the belly feathers, do not carve these, they must appear very soft. Use a bur or gouge to create hills and valleys. For splits cut with a knife as shown on pattern. Stone or burn these feathers. Cut the two long tail feathers together to in sure enough strength. Build up the smaller feathers as shown on the top of the tail, burn these before you glue them together. Insert tail and glue tail coverts.

Insert primaries after the tail is assembled — be creative in your selection of a mount. Remember the area this bird is found and be sure you have the proper leaves, berries, etc., that grow near him.

The legs and feet are again as shown on the pattern, wire, plastic wood, wood.

This is a real beauty. I'm sure your're proud of your endevor. Have patience and you'll have fun.

Keep carving.

GEORGE
Lehman

25

KILLDEER

If you were to see a Killdeer faking a broken wing, while walking in the woods, be very carefull, her young will be near by. There are many birds, both land and water species, that will go through strange antics to keep your attention away from her young. When we observe this type of behavior we leave the area as quickly as possible.

I have wittnessed folks in motor boats chasing loons with their young. Both the drake and the hen will go through the broken wing bit to keep the attention away from their young — I feel sorry for people who have no more to do than torment our wild friends.

This would make a wonderful carving. It has a lot of motion and it tells a story, perhaps you could hide a few of her young behind a stone or log.

These are ideas that come along, and if you are creative enough you can captalize on the incident. There is no need to show what or who is bothering her, this leaves the air of mystery to the viewer to solve.

Some of these sketches are put into stimulate your creative juices — I hope they give you ideas.

Take your time and happy carving.

SCISSOR-TAILED FLYCATCHER

APPROX SIZE 11" to 15"

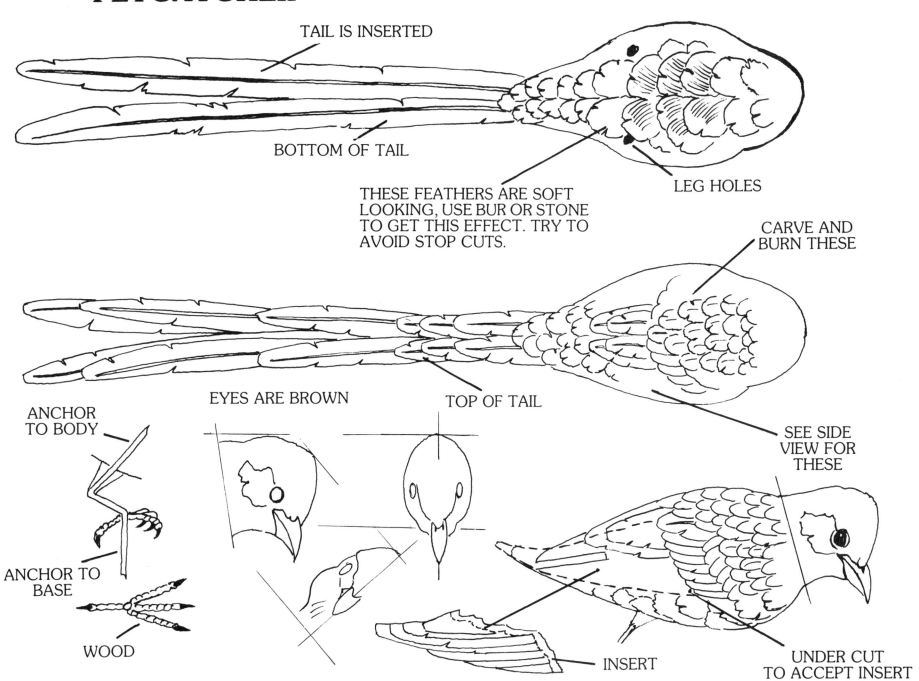

TAIL IS INSERTED

BOTTOM OF TAIL

THESE FEATHERS ARE SOFT LOOKING, USE BUR OR STONE TO GET THIS EFFECT. TRY TO AVOID STOP CUTS.

LEG HOLES

CARVE AND BURN THESE

EYES ARE BROWN

TOP OF TAIL

SEE SIDE VIEW FOR THESE

ANCHOR TO BODY

ANCHOR TO BASE

WOOD

INSERT

UNDER CUT TO ACCEPT INSERT

27

MAC GILLIVRAY'S WARBLER

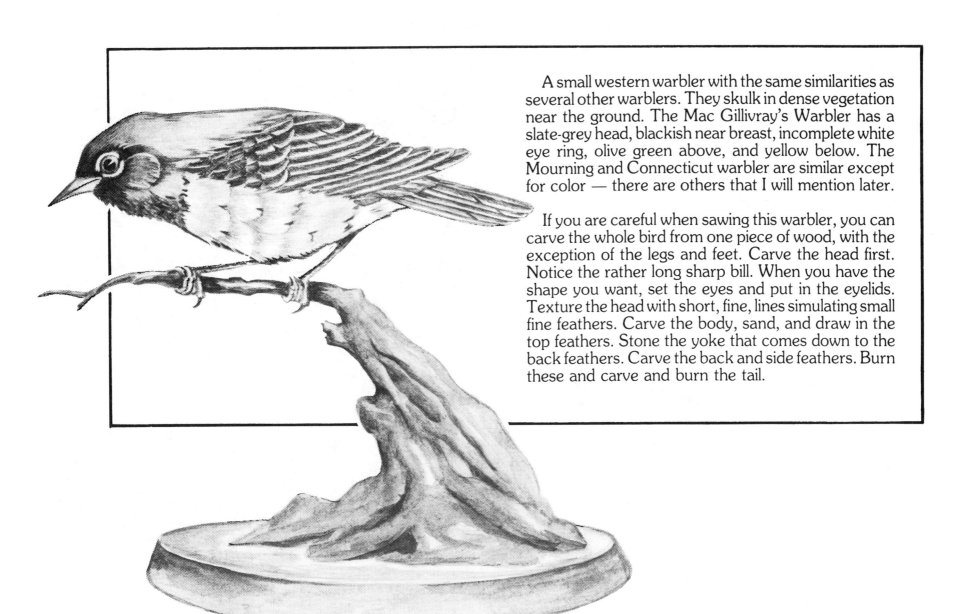

A small western warbler with the same similarities as several other warblers. They skulk in dense vegetation near the ground. The Mac Gillivray's Warbler has a slate-grey head, blackish near breast, incomplete white eye ring, olive green above, and yellow below. The Mourning and Connecticut warbler are similar except for color — there are others that I will mention later.

If you are careful when sawing this warbler, you can carve the whole bird from one piece of wood, with the exception of the legs and feet. Carve the head first. Notice the rather long sharp bill. When you have the shape you want, set the eyes and put in the eyelids. Texture the head with short, fine, lines simulating small fine feathers. Carve the body, sand, and draw in the top feathers. Stone the yoke that comes down to the back feathers. Carve the back and side feathers. Burn these and carve and burn the tail.

The belly feathers are very soft — draw them in and bur the hills and valleys around the feather pattern. Stone the feather texture as shown in the Blue Jay pattern. If these feathers need splits, you can put them in with a sharp exacto knife. This particular warbler can be painted several different ways — to be several different warblers. The feathers and size are the same on three different birds, only the coloring is different. These three are, Mac Gillivray's Warbler, Kentucky Warbler or the Prothonotary Warbler. So depending upon the area you are in, paint the warbler you know best.

Be creative when designing the base for this little beauty. Remember the base can make this well carved warbler a true masterpiece. Be creative and explore the type of leaves or foliage you may want to use, don't over work it! Have fun, be patient, and keep carving.

SPARROW

Kingfisher from "Realism in Wood" showing detail of base . . .

MAC GILLIVRAY'S WARBLER

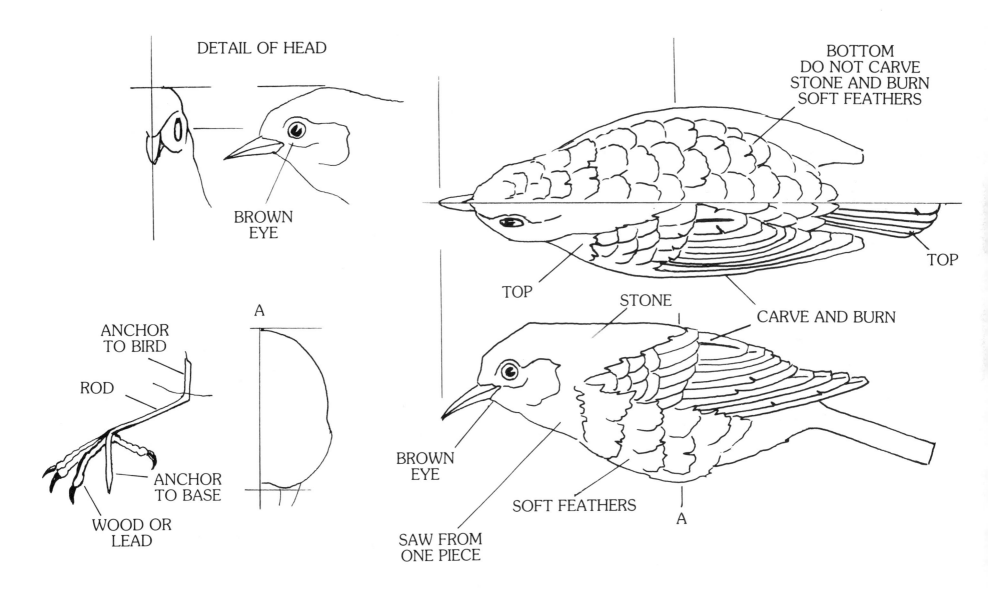

DETAIL OF HEAD

BROWN EYE

BOTTOM
DO NOT CARVE
STONE AND BURN
SOFT FEATHERS

TOP

TOP

STONE

CARVE AND BURN

ANCHOR TO BIRD

ROD

A

ANCHOR TO BASE

WOOD OR LEAD

BROWN EYE

SOFT FEATHERS

SAW FROM ONE PIECE

A

30

EASTERN MEADOWLARK

A stocky brown-streaked bird about 9″ to 11″ long. He has a white edged tail, with a bright yellow throat and breast with a black V. His eyes are brown. He is an american farm bird with a very cheerful song. His habitat usually is the meadows, pastures, and prairies. They normally nest and breed in hayfields.

This is another carving where it would be better to carve the head separate. You need the proper grain for the unusually long pointed beak. Carve the head first. Set the eyes and make the eyelids. Texture the head with very short fine lines simulating small fine feathers. Dowel and glue the head to the rough sawn body. Carve and sand the body. Draw the top feathers, carve and burn these. Leave serveral rows off for the inserts over the tail. Draw the side feathers, carve these and burn again. Carve the secondaires deep enough to accomodate the primary inserts. Carve the tail, glue it into place and insert the top and bottom coverts. Carve and burn the primaries, glue them into place. With plastic wood, patch any spots that are needed. With a low heat iron texture the repairs.

31

Prepare a proper mount for this beauty, be careful not to over-do the base so as to take away from your carving. Keep it simple yet effective. I would suggest that the legs and feet be made from an anchor rod (welding rod), plastic wood and lead (solder) toes. The (solder) lead can be carved very handily to make the toenails and the feet texture.

Take your time and be creative. Have fun and keep carving.

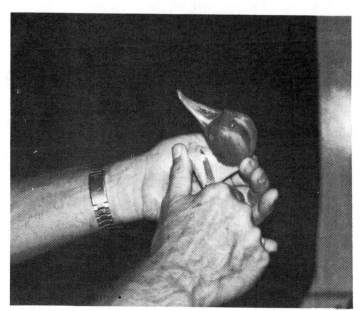

Always carve the head first!

If you can't catch them . . .

carve them!

VESPER SPARROW

32

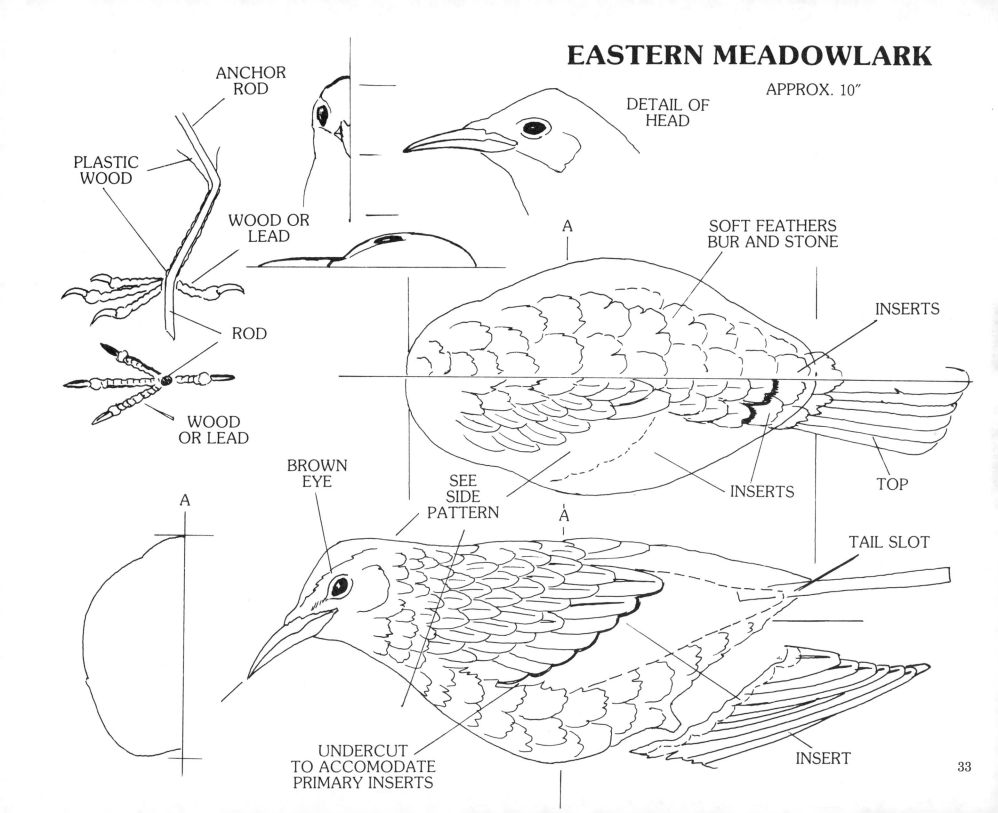

EASTERN MEADOWLARK

APPROX. 10″

ANCHOR ROD

PLASTIC WOOD

WOOD OR LEAD

ROD

WOOD OR LEAD

DETAIL OF HEAD

A

SOFT FEATHERS BUR AND STONE

INSERTS

INSERTS

TOP

BROWN EYE

SEE SIDE PATTERN

A

TAIL SLOT

A

UNDERCUT TO ACCOMODATE PRIMARY INSERTS

INSERT

33

THE BARN SWALLOW

The head of this beauty must be carved separate from the body to get the right grain for strength. Carve the head first! Set the eyes and burn the texture on the head - **do not carve** these feathers. When the head is complete to your satisfaction, dowel and glue it to the rough body. Shape and sand the body. Draw the back pattern, carve, sand and burn these feathers. Leave enough room for tail inserts (see pattern).

Draw in side pattern, carve this to where the secondary feathers end. These must be undercut to accept the primary inserts. Burn the side feathers. Draw in the belly feathers, **do not carve** these, use a small bur or gouge and rough these into hills and valleys. Burn or stone these for a very soft appearance. Insert the tail, insert the tail coverts both top and bottom. Insert the primaries, if these need bending, wet them to prevent splitting.

Select a base and driftwood mount for this beauty. Line up your carving and drill two holes for legs (see pattern). Mount the leg wires into the bird. With plastic wood, build the leg shank into the body. Paint the legs and under side of the bird. Carve the toes and glue them onto the base around the hole —place the bird on the mount, patch any holes with plastic wood. Burn with low heat and paint.

You have only to create some type of base arrangement and this beautiful little Swallow will be done.

Keep carving!

GEORGE
Lehman

34

I was asked to give a seminar on bird carving. When planning this I decided the best approach was a step-by-step chart on carving a bird. Here then is my chart that I prepared to talk from . . .

1. Draw or select a good working pattern.
2. Select a clean, clear piece of wood.
3. If necessary cut the head separate for proper grain.
4. Carve the head first, if this comes out well the rest is easy.
5. Saw side view of body first — if you insert the tail, saw tail slot now.
6. Replace top and bottom wood scraps and saw the top pattern.
7. Dowel and glue head to rough body — after head is carved.
8. Check your pattern from time to time.
9. Keep a centerline on your work at all times.
10. Rough in body — sand! Draw top pattern.
11. Carve top pattern.
12. Draw in one side pattern — carve. (draw and carve one side at a time — handling will tend to erace your pencil lines)
13. When carving is complete, sand entire body so carved feathers blend one into another — before burning.
14. In cases where the feathers appear very soft and not clearly defined — do not carve a hard line, use a gouge or bur to define the feather break, then stone or burn the feathers.
15. Insert tail and insert tail coverts.
16. Prepare mount, mount carving.

Peregrine..

GEORGE
Lehman

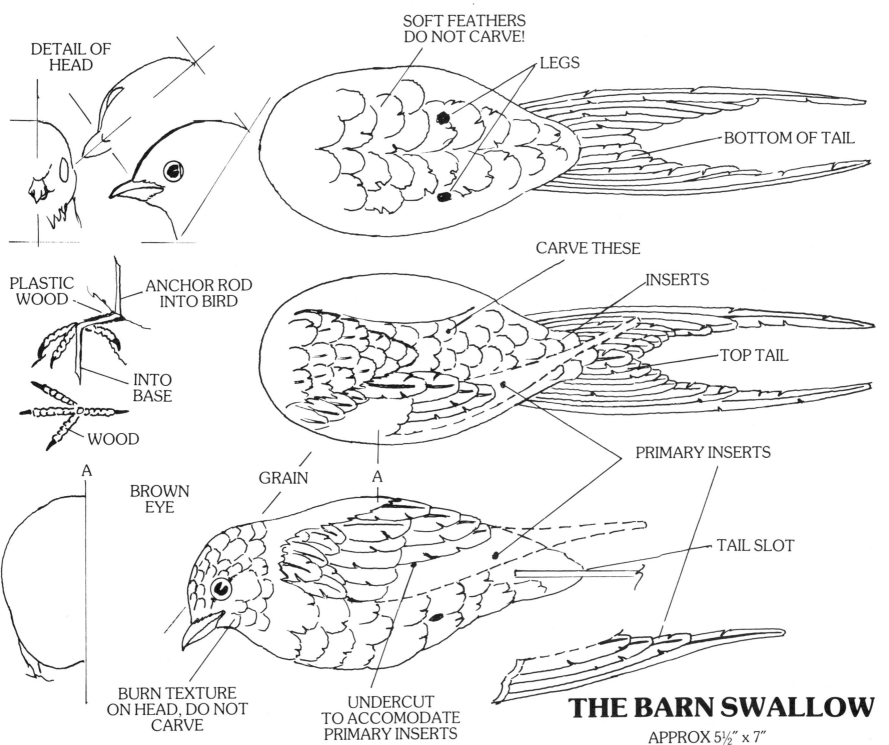

DETAIL OF HEAD

SOFT FEATHERS DO NOT CARVE!

LEGS

BOTTOM OF TAIL

PLASTIC WOOD

ANCHOR ROD INTO BIRD

INTO BASE

WOOD

CARVE THESE

INSERTS

TOP TAIL

PRIMARY INSERTS

TAIL SLOT

A

BROWN EYE

GRAIN

A

BURN TEXTURE ON HEAD, DO NOT CARVE

UNDERCUT TO ACCOMODATE PRIMARY INSERTS

THE BARN SWALLOW

APPROX 5½" x 7"

36

BLACKBURNIAN WARBLER

The Blackburnian Warbler nest in a variety of conifers — spruce, firs, pines and hemlocks. They nest very high and are difficult to see — even though they are brightly colored.

This colorful warbler can be carved from one piece with the exception of the primary inserts. You will note the top and side feathers are carved and burned. The belly feathers are very soft appearing so they must be stoned or burred, do not carve feather stops. The real interesting thing on this bird is the painting after you finish carving him. You will also note the leaves and seeds of the river birch that I have shown, you can use these or create your own background. The fun of any carving is the creating —you can use the pattern, but try to place your subject in unusual positions.

Do not over do your mount so as to take away from your carving.

Have fun, be creative, and above all have patience. Keep carving.

GEORGE
Lehman

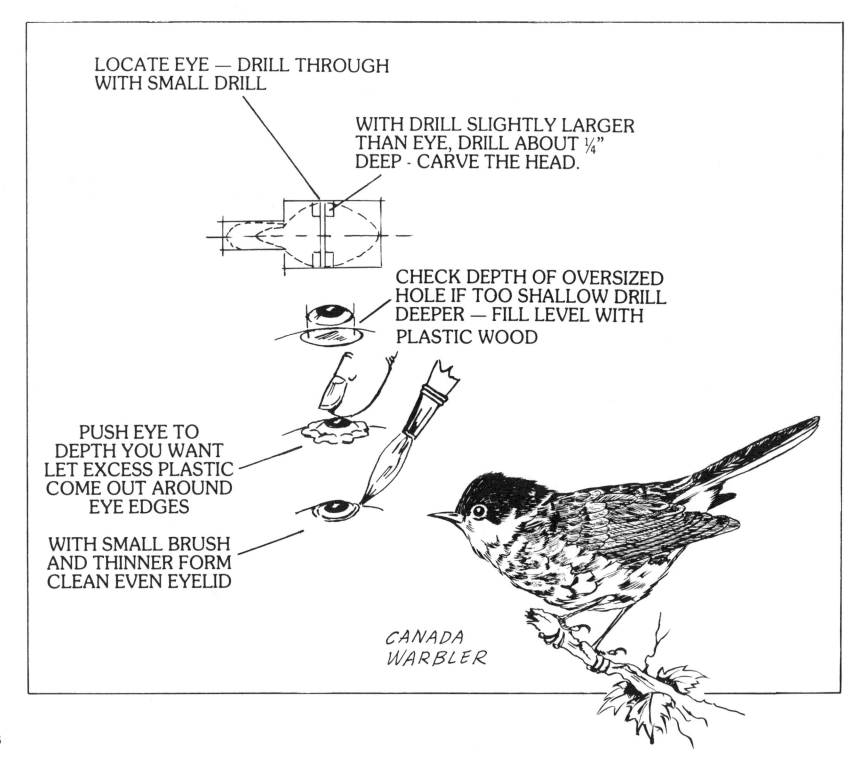

LOCATE EYE — DRILL THROUGH
WITH SMALL DRILL

WITH DRILL SLIGHTLY LARGER
THAN EYE, DRILL ABOUT ¼"
DEEP - CARVE THE HEAD.

CHECK DEPTH OF OVERSIZED
HOLE IF TOO SHALLOW DRILL
DEEPER — FILL LEVEL WITH
PLASTIC WOOD

PUSH EYE TO
DEPTH YOU WANT
LET EXCESS PLASTIC
COME OUT AROUND
EYE EDGES

WITH SMALL BRUSH
AND THINNER FORM
CLEAN EVEN EYELID

CANADA
WARBLER

BLACKBURNIAN WARBLER

APPROX 5″ in LENTH

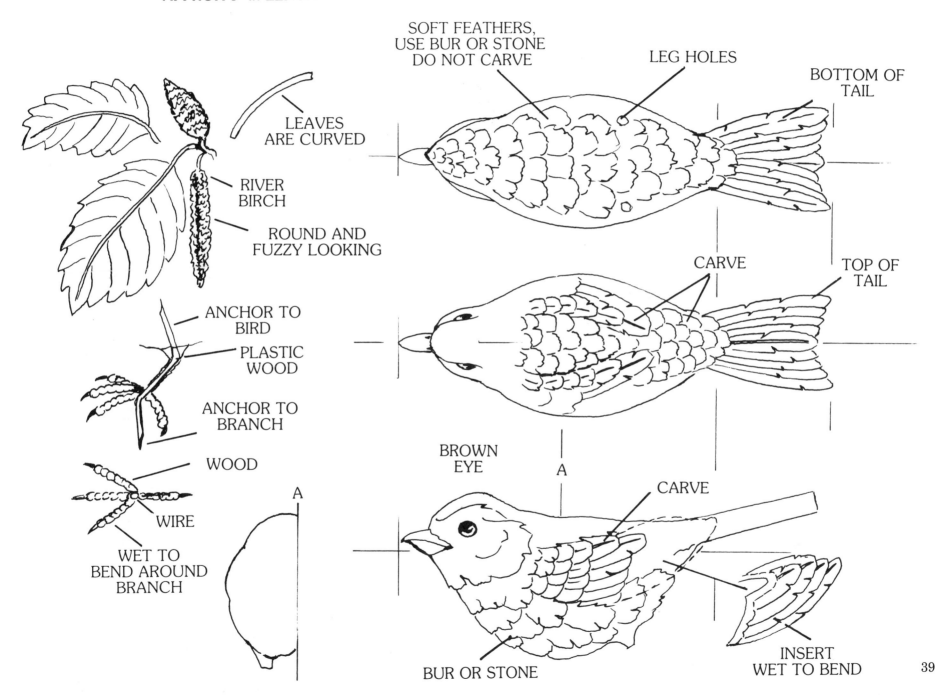

LEAVES
ARE CURVED

RIVER
BIRCH

ROUND AND
FUZZY LOOKING

ANCHOR TO
BIRD

PLASTIC
WOOD

ANCHOR TO
BRANCH

WOOD

WIRE

WET TO
BEND AROUND
BRANCH

A

SOFT FEATHERS,
USE BUR OR STONE
DO NOT CARVE

LEG HOLES

BOTTOM OF
TAIL

CARVE

TOP OF
TAIL

BROWN
EYE

A

CARVE

BUR OR STONE

INSERT
WET TO BEND

39

SCARLET TANAGER

A brilliant scarlet bird with black wings and tail. His habitat is the mature woodland, especially oak and pine. He ranges from southeast Canada, east central United States to Columbia and Bolivia in winter.

This beauty should be cut head and body separate, because of the wood grain. The tail and tail coverts and the primaries are all inserts. Carve the head first! If this comes out well, the rest seems to fall into place. When you have the head shaped the way you want it, set in the eyes — they are brown. Use your iron to texture the head with very short fine strokes to simulate small fine feathers. Draw in the top feathers, carve and burn these. Draw in the side feathers, carve and burn these. Undercut the secondary feathers to accomodate the primary inserts as shown on pattern. The belly feathers are soft, so do not carve these — draw them. Bur in hills and valleys and stone the texture as shown on the Blue Jay page. Carve the tail and burn both sides before you insert. When the tail is glued into place, insert the tail coverts, both top and bottom.

Select a piece of driftwood to mount your masterpiece. Use your creative talents and design an attractive piece. The legs and feet are as shown on pattern. For small bird feet I prefer to use lead for the toes, it is easily carved and textured and bends to fit any mount. For good results, buy a solder roll without the acid core, it works real well.

Have fun, keep carving and don't hurry — patience is the key to good carving.

BLACKBURNIAN WARBLER...

Owl and Mouse from "Realism in Wood"

SCARLET TANAGER

APPROX. 7"

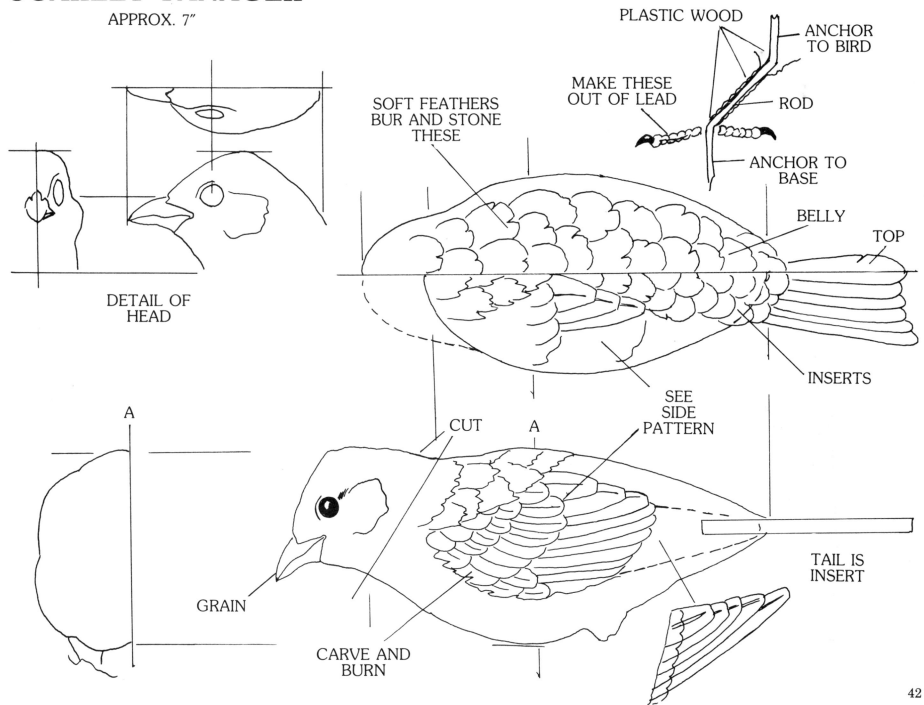

DETAIL OF HEAD

PLASTIC WOOD

ANCHOR TO BIRD

MAKE THESE OUT OF LEAD

ROD

ANCHOR TO BASE

SOFT FEATHERS BUR AND STONE THESE

BELLY

TOP

INSERTS

SEE SIDE PATTERN

A

CUT

A

GRAIN

CARVE AND BURN

TAIL IS INSERT

RED POLL

The Red Polls are members of the huge finch and sparrow family. They will stay in the north woods as long as the food supply holds out. They prefer the seeds of the Birch, Alder and Elm to any other food.

I would suggest carving the head separate from the body to gain the strength of proper grain in the wood. (see pattern) Finish the head first. Insert the eyes and make the eyelids. Burn the feather texture on the head. Rough carve the body and dowel. Glue and put the head on the body. (You may want to turn the head for a little action) When this is dry, carve the body and neck to the desired shape. Sand and trace the back pattern on — Carve and burn these feathers. Trace the side pattern on and carve these. You will note you must undercut the secondaries to accomodate the primary inserts. Before you put in the primaries, carve the tail, top and bottom.

Bur or stone the belly feathers (as shown). Glue the primaries in and fill any cracks with plastic wood. Burn in the texture with a **low** heat.

Select a suitable mount for the Red Poll. Deside what type of foliage you want to use (if any). Drill two leg holes in the bird, insert 1/16 leg wires, bend and fit them as you want. Drill the base and glue the legs and bird to the mount. Carve the toes and glue them in the proper place. If you need to bend these to fit around the base, wet them to keep from splitting. Fill in any holes or cracks with plastic wood and let dry.

Most of us have seen Red Polls so the painting should be no problem. Good luck, have fun and keep carving.

Lehman

This is the way I usually insert the tail coverts. I would suggest, unless in extreme cases, never leaving more than three or four rows to insert. Start your first row far enough down on the tail so the bend in the feather will not be too sharp. When the first row is glued and dry, sand the edges so they blend right into the tail feathers. Whenever you sand a section touch up the sanded area with your iron.

On the second row be sure the inserted feather covers the first ones (much like shingles on a roof) allow these to dry and again sand the edges. Touch up your sanded areas with a burning iron.

The third and last inserts are the crucial ones. In order to insure a near perfect fit, I make a paper pattern of each feather to be inserted. Use a small piece of thin paper and with a soft lead pencil make a pattern of the existing edge of the feather on the bird. Transfer this pattern on very thin wood, cut it out, test it and trim where necessary. When you have a good fit, glue the first feather. Smooth off the edges so the second will fit as well. Proceed to do this with each feather until you have completed the tail coverts. Let these dry - sand the body feathers so they flow smoothly into the tail coverts. If you have any defects a small amount of plastic wood will seal them. Burn the sanded parts. If you have had to use plastic wood, be sure to use low heat to touch this up.

The real secret in a good looking insert, is the sanding and smoothing of the feathers to accept the next one and so on.

I hope this is clear. This will apply to the wing coverts as well.

It's really very easy once you get the idea that each feather lies flat against the other.

Have fun!

GEORGE
Lehman

44

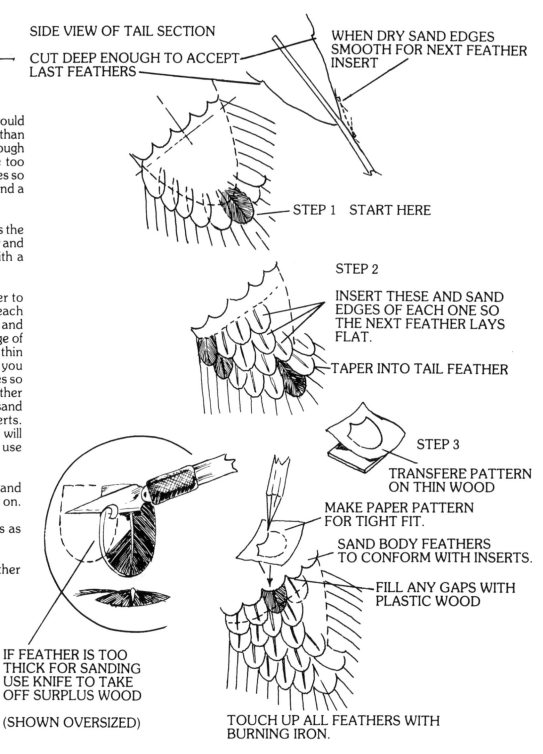

SIDE VIEW OF TAIL SECTION

CUT DEEP ENOUGH TO ACCEPT LAST FEATHERS

WHEN DRY SAND EDGES SMOOTH FOR NEXT FEATHER INSERT

STEP 1   START HERE

STEP 2

INSERT THESE AND SAND EDGES OF EACH ONE SO THE NEXT FEATHER LAYS FLAT.

TAPER INTO TAIL FEATHER

STEP 3

TRANSFERE PATTERN ON THIN WOOD

MAKE PAPER PATTERN FOR TIGHT FIT.

SAND BODY FEATHERS TO CONFORM WITH INSERTS.

FILL ANY GAPS WITH PLASTIC WOOD

IF FEATHER IS TOO THICK FOR SANDING USE KNIFE TO TAKE OFF SURPLUS WOOD

(SHOWN OVERSIZED)

TOUCH UP ALL FEATHERS WITH BURNING IRON.

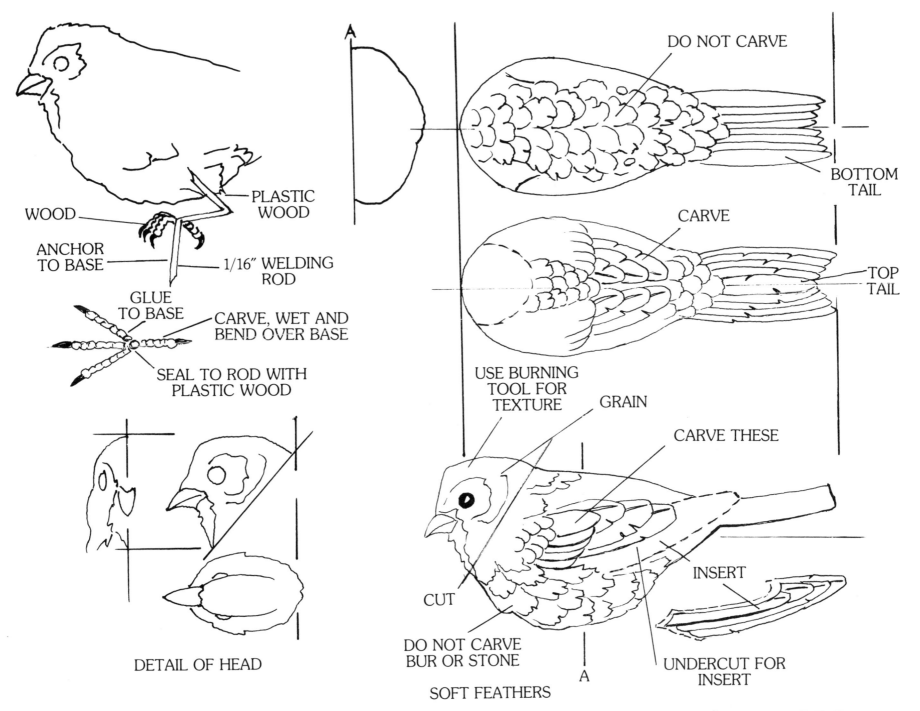

PLASTIC WOOD

WOOD

ANCHOR TO BASE

1/16" WELDING ROD

GLUE TO BASE

CARVE, WET AND BEND OVER BASE

SEAL TO ROD WITH PLASTIC WOOD

DETAIL OF HEAD

A

DO NOT CARVE

BOTTOM TAIL

CARVE

TOP TAIL

USE BURNING TOOL FOR TEXTURE

GRAIN

CARVE THESE

INSERT

CUT

DO NOT CARVE BUR OR STONE

SOFT FEATHERS

A

UNDERCUT FOR INSERT

RED POLL

45

GREAT CRESTED FLYCATCHER

A rather large, 9" inches, bird with brown above, gray throat, yellow belly and slightly crested head. He habitats the open forest, orchards, and large trees in farm country. He ranges from southern Canada to the Gulf of Mexico. He is the only eastern Flycatcher to nest in holes. He occasionally uses shed snake-skins for nest lining.

This beauty again must be cut from two pieces of wood, because of the grain needed for the rather long sharp bill. Carve the head first (note the semi tufted crest) for that special effect on the crest a stone would work well. Set the eyes, form the eyelids. If you want the bill open, as the pattern shows, remove the bottom bill with a sharp exacto knife — hollow out both the top and bottom, paint and reglue the bottom bill in place. When you are happy with the head, dowel and glue it to the rough body. You may want to turn the head slightly to give the bird a little action.

Carve the body and sand. Draw the top pattern, carve and burn. Draw the side pattern, carve and burn. Allow an undercut to accept the primary inserts as shown. Before you glue the primary inserts, carve and burn the tail. Glue into place and insert the tail coverts. Now glue the primary inserts, use plastic wood to patch any imperfections. With low heat iron touch up all patch work. The feet and legs again should be a rod (for leg and anchor) lead (carve solder) for feet and nails, plastic wood for patch work and leg texture. As I have said so many times before, be creative when selecting a base for your Flycatcher to sit on. Perhaps an apple blossom with leaves on a piece of apple wood.

Have fun, take your time, be creative and keep carving.

CHICKADEE

FINCHES

The Owl and the Mouse

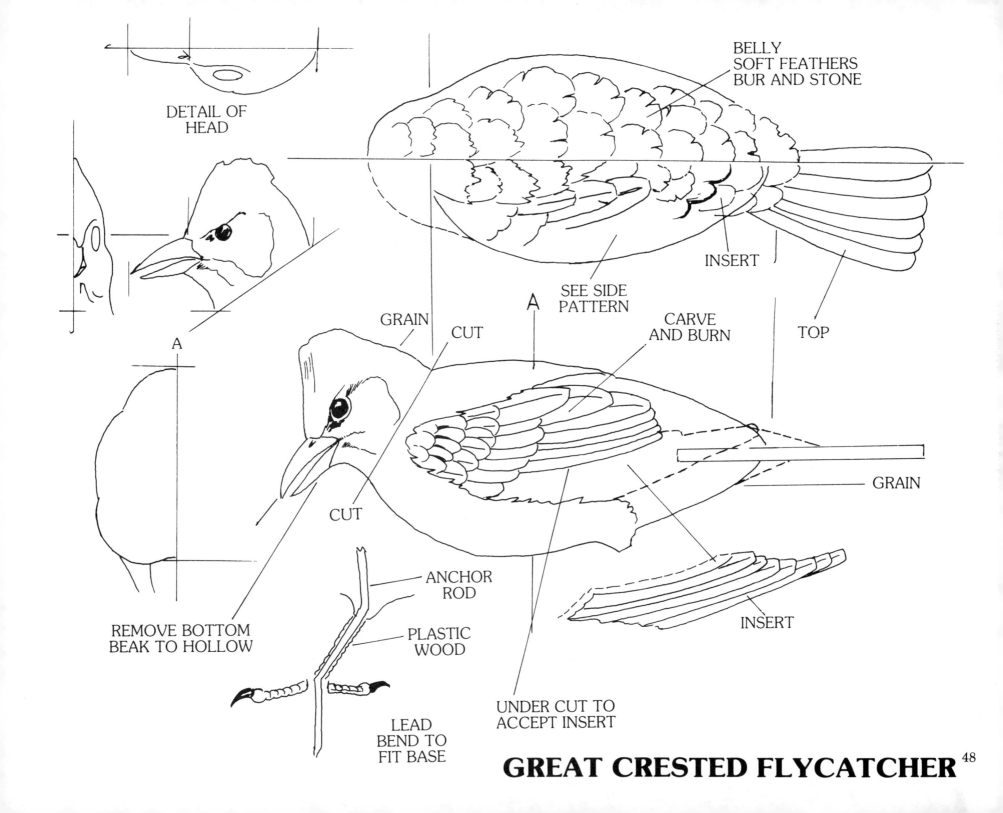

DETAIL OF
HEAD

BELLY
SOFT FEATHERS
BUR AND STONE

INSERT

SEE SIDE
PATTERN

A

GRAIN

CUT

A

CARVE
AND BURN

TOP

CUT

GRAIN

INSERT

REMOVE BOTTOM
BEAK TO HOLLOW

ANCHOR
ROD

PLASTIC
WOOD

UNDER CUT TO
ACCEPT INSERT

LEAD
BEND TO
FIT BASE

GREAT CRESTED FLYCATCHER 48

CARDINAL

The Cardinal's rich colors makes him easy to spot — he can be found in open woods, forest edges, thickets, suburbs and parks. He will readily come to feeders.

This beauty can be carved from one piece of wood if you desire. Saw the pattern slightly oversized. Carve the head first. Remove the bottom bill and hollow out, insert berry as shown on pattern, glue back in place. Stone the hood and burn the head. Now proceed to rough carve the body. Sand very carefully and draw in the back feathers, carve and burn.

Draw in the side feathers, carve these, burn both sides of primaries where they show from both sides.

Carve the tail, sand and burn. Draw the belly feathers. (these are very soft) Use no knife stops on these, bur or stone these, make feather splits with a knife.

Select a piece of driftwood to mount your Cardinal on. This is the time to be creative. Be sure the leaves and wood you use are of the area a Cardinal lives.

Use the same proceedure as shown for the legs and feet. Wire plastic wood sealer and wood toes. You should be very proud of this beauty. Have fun,

keep carving.

GEORGE
Lehman

49

I have put more line drawings from my sketch book into this book. I felt that you creative carvers could use some of these to design your own patterns —

I'm sure you would rather have new ideas rather than photos of my works. The satisfaction of creating a carving, regardless of the pattern you use, is in the way you mount it. Change the wing position or the way you've placed the head.

Just the smallest amount of creative planning can make your carving a real masterpiece.

Many times I'll consult my wife before I mount a bird on its driftwood base. She can see things that I have missed — it helps to have constructive critizism.

One of our greatest assets is the carving clubs that have developed all over the country. If you don't belong — join. The members are so friendly, and always willing to help with questions you may have.

You can also be of great help to some one else who may have some unanswered questions. It's a good feeling to be able to give of your talent.

Keep carving and
make friends —

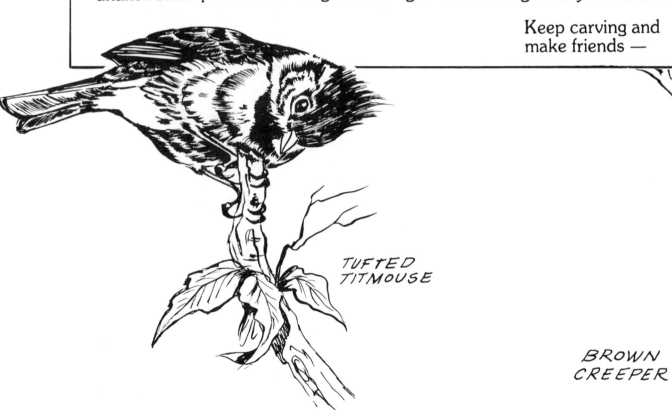

TUFTED
TITMOUSE

BROWN
CREEPER

CARDINAL

APPROX 7" to 8"

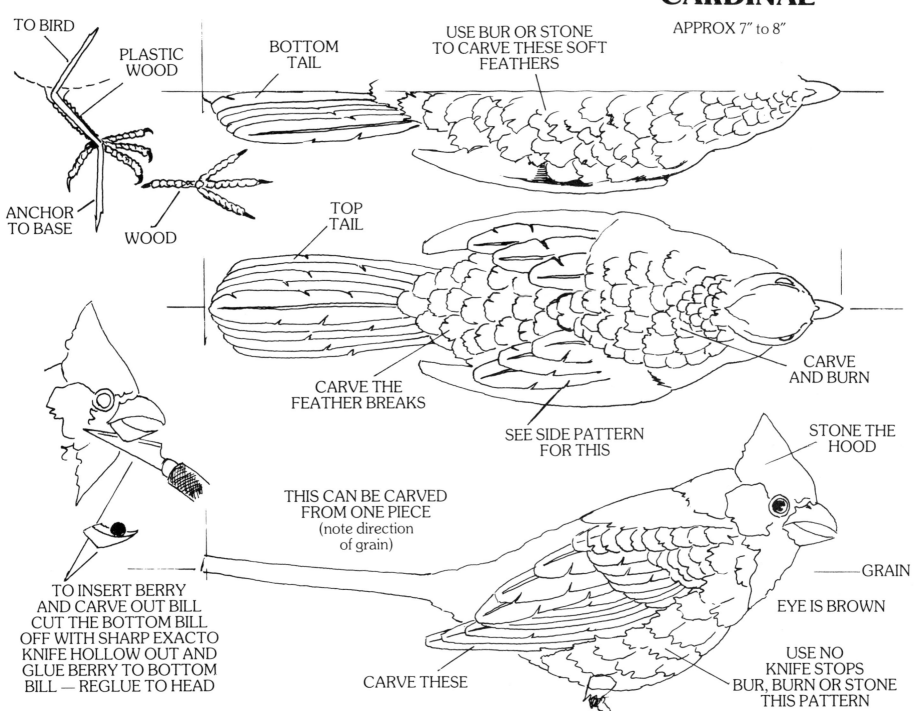

TO BIRD

PLASTIC WOOD

ANCHOR TO BASE

WOOD

BOTTOM TAIL

USE BUR OR STONE TO CARVE THESE SOFT FEATHERS

TOP TAIL

CARVE THE FEATHER BREAKS

SEE SIDE PATTERN FOR THIS

CARVE AND BURN

STONE THE HOOD

THIS CAN BE CARVED FROM ONE PIECE
(note direction of grain)

TO INSERT BERRY AND CARVE OUT BILL CUT THE BOTTOM BILL OFF WITH SHARP EXACTO KNIFE HOLLOW OUT AND GLUE BERRY TO BOTTOM BILL — REGLUE TO HEAD

CARVE THESE

GRAIN

EYE IS BROWN

USE NO KNIFE STOPS BUR, BURN OR STONE THIS PATTERN

51

YELLOW HEADED BLACK BIRD

A beautiful song bird. He can be found nesting over water 2 to 4 feet deep. The nests are slung between reed stems and are woven of soggy blades of dead grass. This again must be a separate head to gain the strength of the proper grain in the rather long bill. The head should be carved first. Pay attention to the pattern on this one. To open the bill and hollow it out, use the same technique as was used on the Cardinal and Evening Grosbeak. The carving is basically the same as I have been describing in the other patterns.

Lets take a few minutes to describe what I mean by soft feathers and stoning. When I say **"do not carve"**, I mean that there should be no feather stops or cuts, each feather or group of feathers are designated by a bump and valley as shown on the following sketch. Then the texture is put in with a small stone and power tool. The splits in the feathers are cut in with a knife before you burn or stone the feathers. When you carve the feathers they too should be sanded so each feather rounds off to fit into the next one, like shingles on a house — but not quiet so uniform.

You will note the pattern of the Black bird is in a slightly different position than the halftone drawing. I did this to challenge your creativity — let's see what you can do with this beauty.

Have fun and take your time, keep carving!

YOUNG ROBIN

This Cardinal is a good example of "soft feathers" on it's belly — as described in the Blue Jay pattern . . .

GEORGE
Lehman

YELLOW HEADED BLACK BIRD

APPROX 8" x 11"

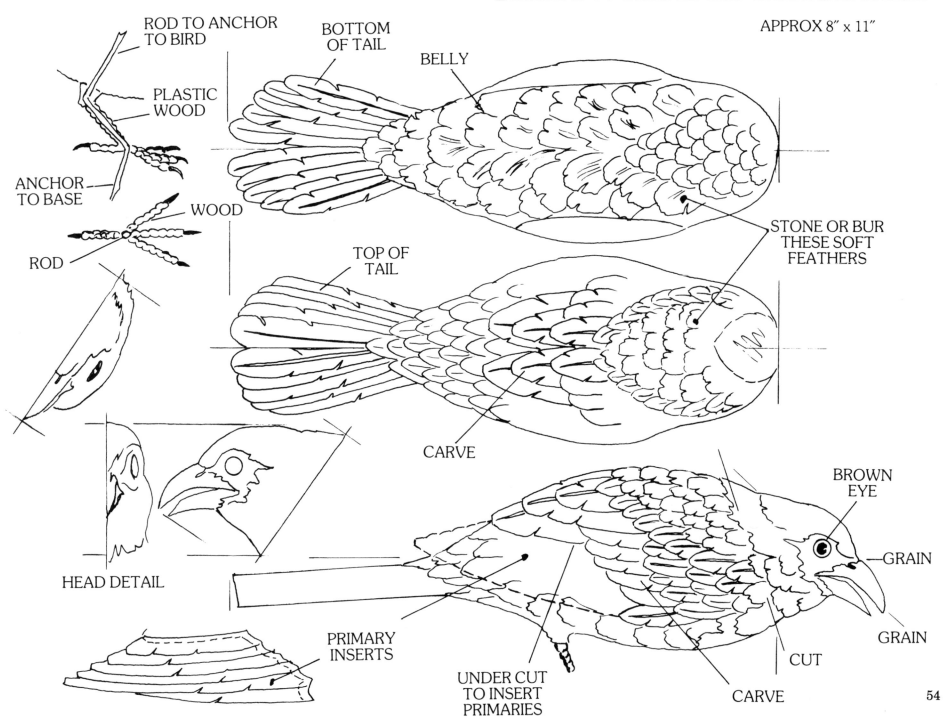

ROD TO ANCHOR
TO BIRD

PLASTIC
WOOD

ANCHOR
TO BASE

ROD

WOOD

BOTTOM
OF TAIL

BELLY

STONE OR BUR
THESE SOFT
FEATHERS

TOP OF
TAIL

CARVE

HEAD DETAIL

PRIMARY
INSERTS

UNDER CUT
TO INSERT
PRIMARIES

CARVE

BROWN
EYE

GRAIN

GRAIN

CUT

54

THE GREATER ROADRUNNER

A Western, desert bird that would rather run than fly — streamlined, with a long tail and very strong legs. He has been clocked with speeds up to 15 miles per hour.

Carve the head separate, use a bur or stone to get the texture of the unrully tuft on his head. When the head is completely carved, insert the eyes, dowel and glue the head to the roughed in body. You may want to turn the head slightly to give some realistic action to your carving. Carve the body and sand very carefully — trace the top pattern, carve the feathers (not too deep) sand all the feathers so one tapers into the next. It would be a good idea to burn these and the head. This will let you see what your finished bird will look like. Draw the side pattern and carve. Where the primaries insert you must under cut (see pattern). This is true on the tail coverts as well. Burn both sides and draw the belly feathers. **Do not** carve these, use a small bur or stone and rough the edges of each penciled feather. Sand this very carefully — you should now have a series of hills and valleys — burn the feather texture. Split some of the feathers for realism. Carve the Tail, glue into the body, insert tall coverts as shown. Carve the primaries, fit and burn them before you glue them. If the bend is great you may have to wet the piece to keep from splitting. Glue primaries into place, pin or tape until dry. The legs and feet remain. Use a sturdy piece of rod to anchor this bird, the top or flank of the leg is wood, the toes are also wood glued to the base in their proper place (note the toes are two in front and two in back) fill any gaps with plastic wood. Your creative talents can now be put to use mounting the Roadrunner in a desert atmosphere. The mounting is just as important as your carving. Have fun and keep carving.

Townsend's Warbler..

Putting the final touches on the Cheetah carving . . .

56

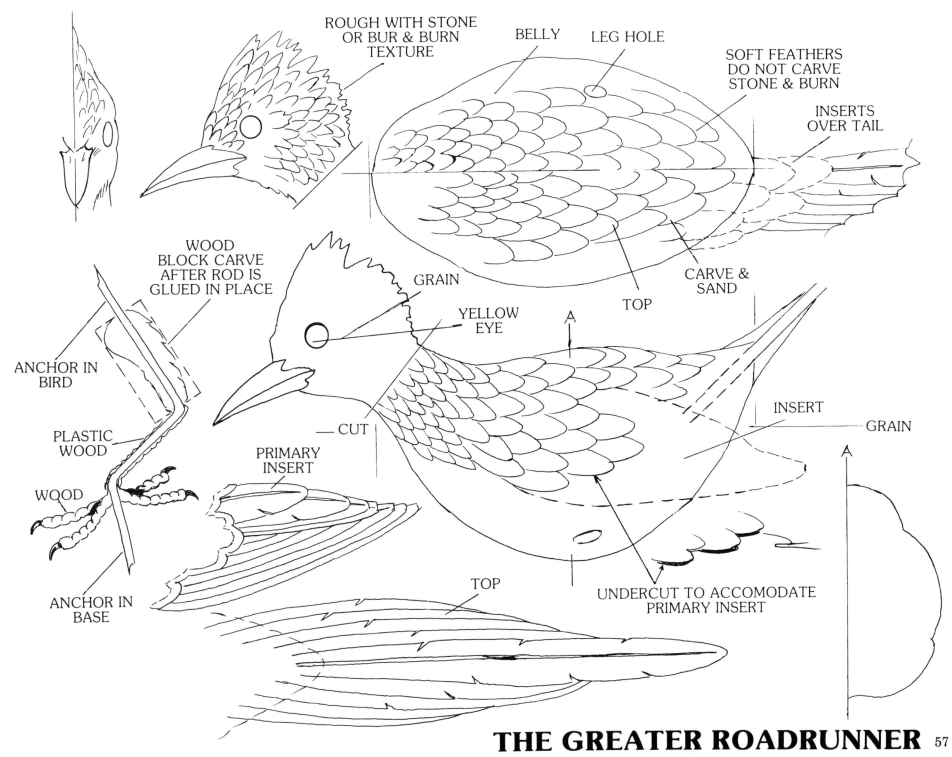

ROUGH WITH STONE OR BUR & BURN TEXTURE

BELLY

LEG HOLE

SOFT FEATHERS DO NOT CARVE STONE & BURN

INSERTS OVER TAIL

CARVE & SAND

TOP

WOOD BLOCK CARVE AFTER ROD IS GLUED IN PLACE

GRAIN

YELLOW EYE

ANCHOR IN BIRD

PLASTIC WOOD

WOOD

CUT

PRIMARY INSERT

A

INSERT

GRAIN

A

ANCHOR IN BASE

TOP

UNDERCUT TO ACCOMODATE PRIMARY INSERT

THE GREATER ROADRUNNER 57

APPROX SIZE 20" to 24"

HOUSE WRENS

The House Wrens are a small energetic gray-brown bird. They range from Canada to Argentina and can be found in open woods, towns, gardens and many nest in houses we supply for them.

Cut the two birds out as shown. I've inserted the tail on both to have the proper grain, and avoid any chance of breaking.

You will note that one head is turned slightly, this will give a little action in your carving. Carve the heads first; you will note the bills are slightly curved. When you are satisfied with the heads, proceed to carve the bodies, sand and draw in the feather patterns. I burned the top feathers in rather than carve them — it worked very well for me. This is optional, I carved the wings however and I inserted the primaries.

Before you put your primaries in, carve the tail and glue it in place, seal the tail with plastic wood and burn to conform with the body pattern.

Select a piece of driftwood for your pair of wrens. Use 1/16" rod for legs (as shown on pattern). Mount your birds and build up the feet with either lead or plastic wood. Let dry and carve the toes to look as real as possible.

I hope you have enjoyed carving these two little gems. Have fun painting these wrens and keep carving.

CHICKADEE

Here are two examples of mounting where it gets a little harder to figure out —

The Chicadee hanging on that very small weed is done this way. First, the weed is a welding rod (strong enough to hold the bird without bending too much. A slight sway is fine, that will give it a lot of realism and motion. Second, take two small rods for the legs, drill into the Chicadee body, glue them. With a small torch, silver solder the legs to the stem.

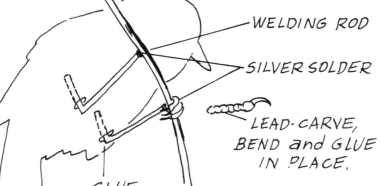

WELDING ROD

SILVER SOLDER

LEAD-CARVE, BEND and GLUE IN PLACE.

GLUE

Then, as in the diagram, make the feet out of coreless solder and glue to the rod. Cover the legs with plastic wood and burn the texture with a low heat iron.

The second drawing shows a Warbler clutching grass — the same procedure is used, however, to simulate the grass — flatten out the rod and and again silver solder the legs as in drawing.

BLACKPOLL WARBLER

HOUSE WRENS

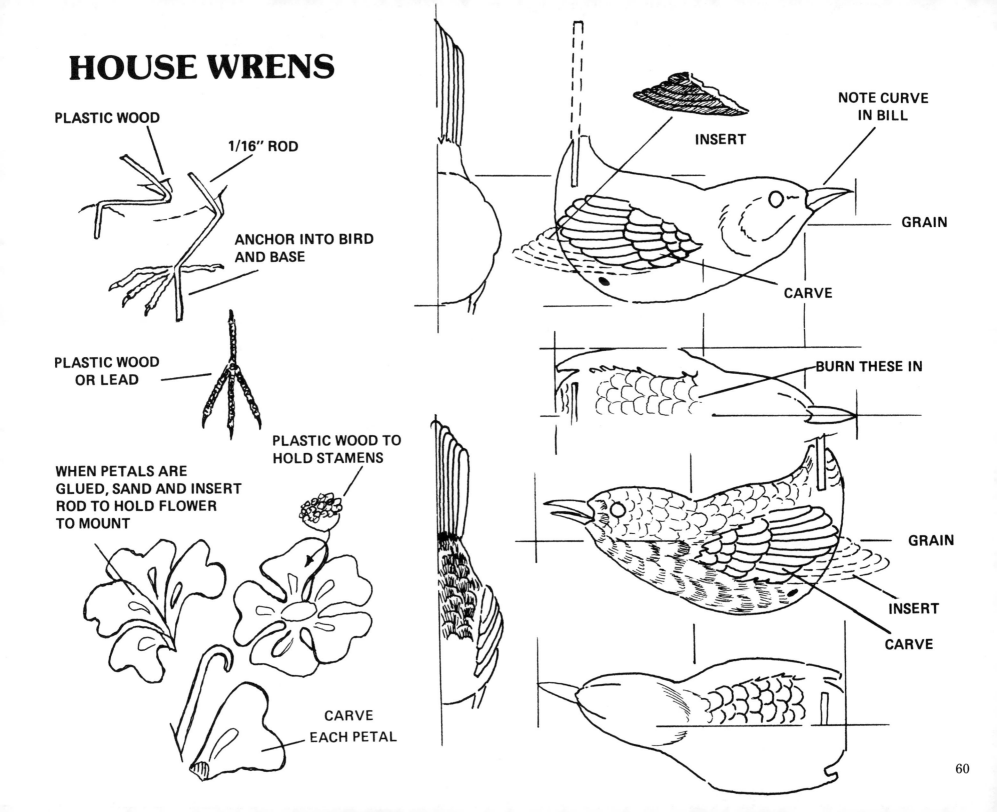

PLASTIC WOOD

1/16" ROD

ANCHOR INTO BIRD AND BASE

PLASTIC WOOD OR LEAD

WHEN PETALS ARE GLUED, SAND AND INSERT ROD TO HOLD FLOWER TO MOUNT

PLASTIC WOOD TO HOLD STAMENS

CARVE EACH PETAL

INSERT

NOTE CURVE IN BILL

GRAIN

CARVE

BURN THESE IN

GRAIN

INSERT

CARVE

60

AMERICAN GOLDFINCH

American Goldfinch, about 5″ long, beautifully colored with his bright yellow and black body combination. His body is yellow and white, and his wings and tail are black and white. He has a clear canary like song and can be found most everywhere in the U.S and southern Canada.

I cut the head and body of this beauty out of one piece of wood — leaving the tail and the wing sections as inserts. Select a good clear piece of basswood 2″ x 3″ x 4½″. Saw the pattern out slightly oversized giving yourself extra wood to work with. Carve the head first. When you have that just the way you want it, drill and set the eyes using plastic wood to form the eyelids (see page on setting eyes).

Rough carve the body, when you have it shaped and sanded, draw the top pattern — these feathers are "soft" do not carve stops for these. See page on making soft feathers. When you have these stoned, draw the side pattern, carve the feathers indicated and under cut them to accept the primary and secondary inserts. Burn the texture into the back and sides.

LONG-EARED OWL

MARTIN

When they are glued and put into place, a good way to hold them until they dry is to wrap string around the bird, holding the primaries tight to the body.

Your next step and a very important one is to prepare a mount for your bird — keep it simple and not too large —you can be creative on this. When you have selected the mount, drill two holes into the bird and attach the leg wires. Proceed to make the feet (see page on feet). I would suggest using the carved solder toes and plastic wood the leg and shank.

You should be very proud of this beauty — now painting is not too tough on this one. Have fun, keep carving.

Proceed to draw the belly feathers. These again are very soft feathers and should be stoned for texture. Carve the tail — curve it slightly and burn the texture into it before you attach it to the body. Glue it into place and insert the tail coverts. Now carve the primary and secondary inserts — you will note the pattern has allowed extra wood to slide under the feathers you have carved. If you need to bend these to fit be sure and wet them to keep them from splitting.

AMERICAN GOLDFINCH

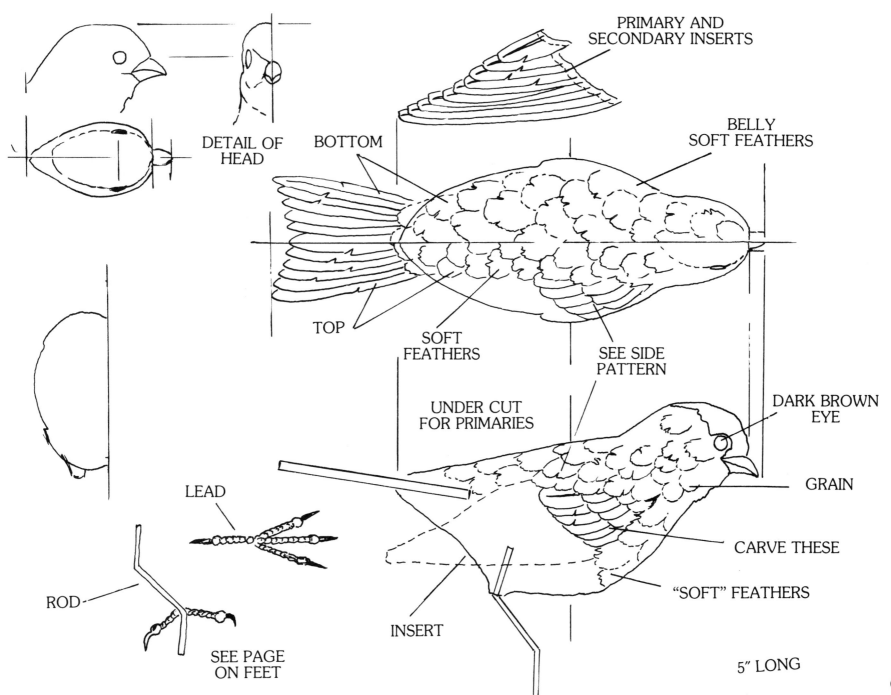

DETAIL OF HEAD

PRIMARY AND SECONDARY INSERTS

BOTTOM

BELLY SOFT FEATHERS

TOP

SOFT FEATHERS

SEE SIDE PATTERN

UNDER CUT FOR PRIMARIES

DARK BROWN EYE

GRAIN

CARVE THESE

LEAD

"SOFT" FEATHERS

ROD

INSERT

SEE PAGE ON FEET

5" LONG

WILD ANIMALS
for your creative
CARVING...

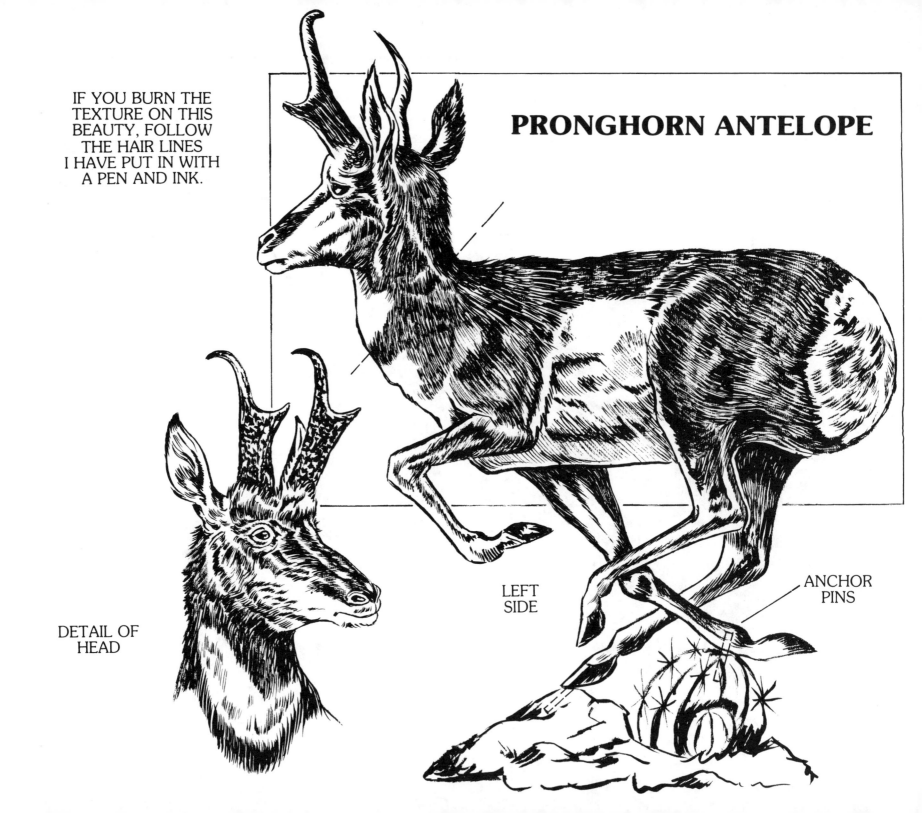

IF YOU BURN THE
TEXTURE ON THIS
BEAUTY, FOLLOW
THE HAIR LINES
I HAVE PUT IN WITH
A PEN AND INK.

PRONGHORN ANTELOPE

DETAIL OF
HEAD

LEFT
SIDE

ANCHOR
PINS

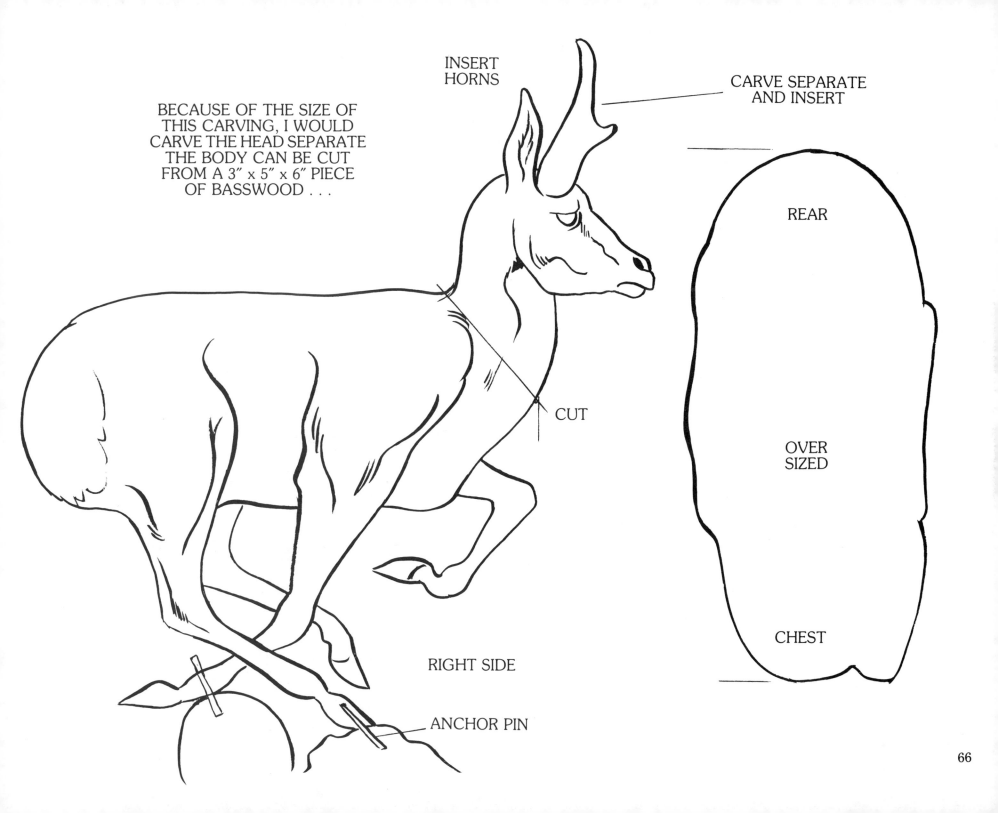

INSERT
HORNS

CARVE SEPARATE
AND INSERT

BECAUSE OF THE SIZE OF
THIS CARVING, I WOULD
CARVE THE HEAD SEPARATE
THE BODY CAN BE CUT
FROM A 3″ x 5″ x 6″ PIECE
OF BASSWOOD . . .

REAR

CUT

OVER
SIZED

RIGHT SIDE

CHEST

ANCHOR PIN

66

CANADIAN LYNX

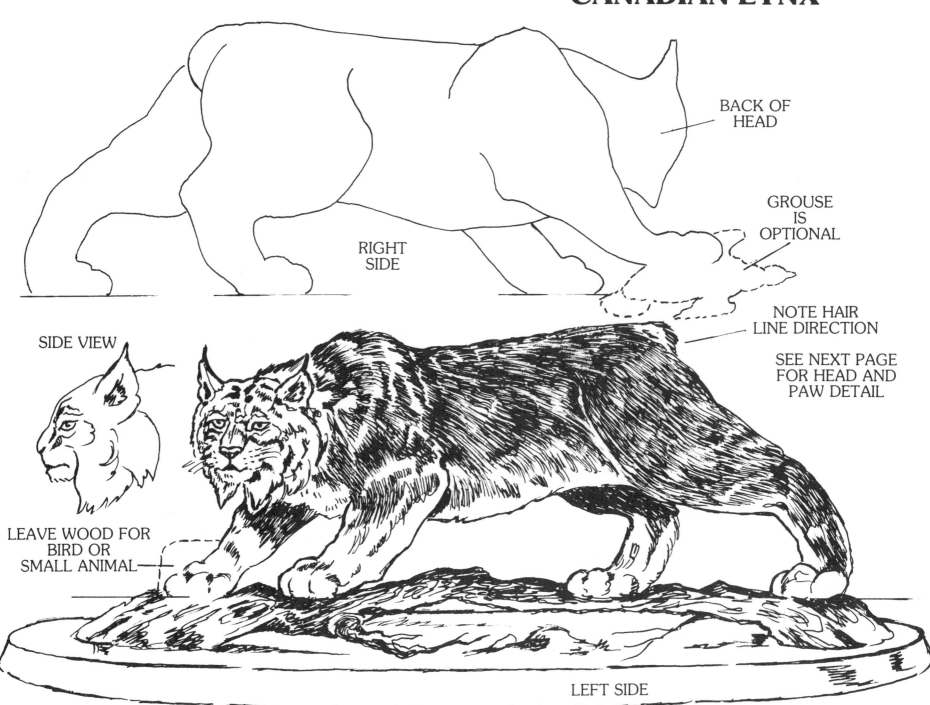

BACK OF HEAD

GROUSE IS OPTIONAL

RIGHT SIDE

NOTE HAIR LINE DIRECTION

SEE NEXT PAGE FOR HEAD AND PAW DETAIL

SIDE VIEW

LEAVE WOOD FOR BIRD OR SMALL ANIMAL

LEFT SIDE

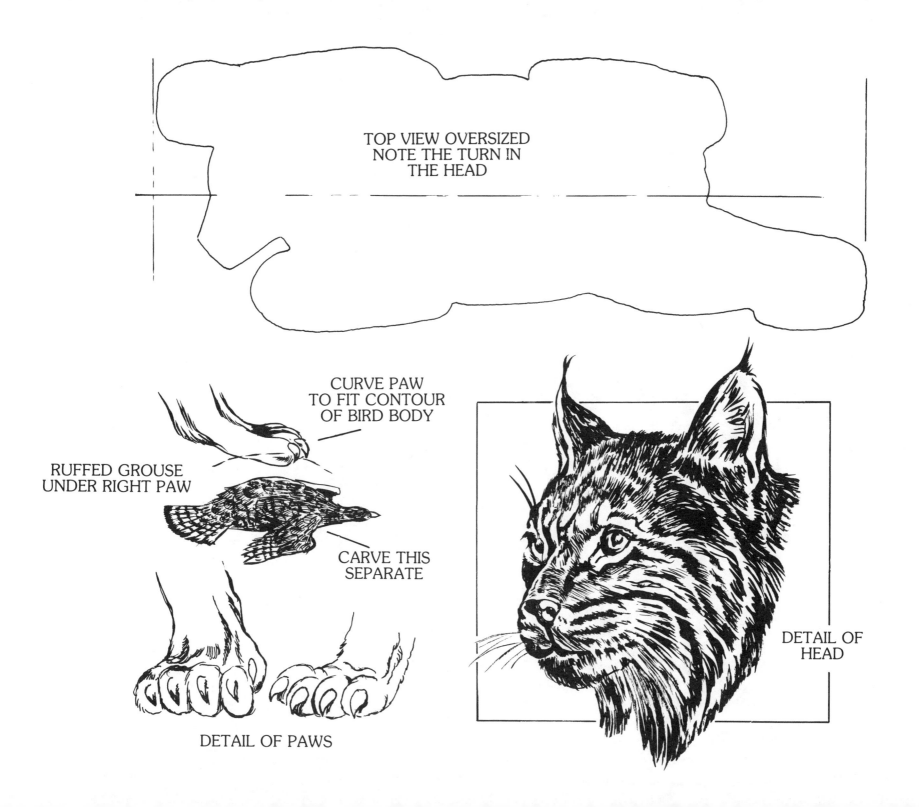

TOP VIEW OVERSIZED
NOTE THE TURN IN
THE HEAD

CURVE PAW
TO FIT CONTOUR
OF BIRD BODY

RUFFED GROUSE
UNDER RIGHT PAW

CARVE THIS
SEPARATE

DETAIL OF PAWS

DETAIL OF
HEAD

68

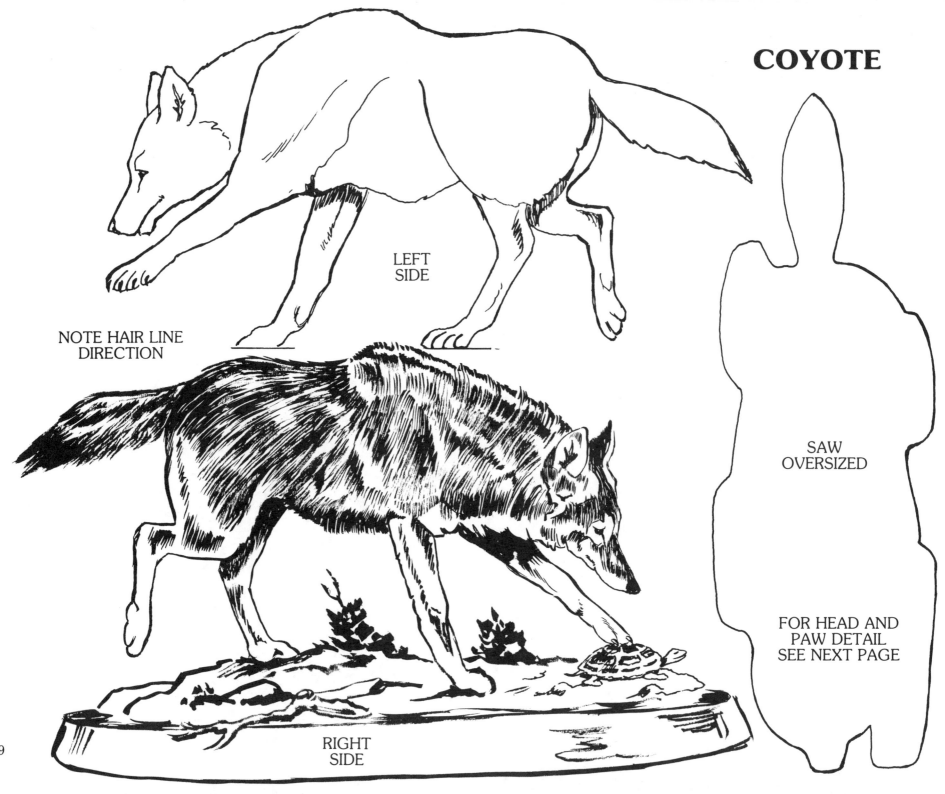

COYOTE

LEFT
SIDE

NOTE HAIR LINE
DIRECTION

RIGHT
SIDE

SAW
OVERSIZED

FOR HEAD AND
PAW DETAIL
SEE NEXT PAGE

69

THE COYOTE'S EARS ARE LARGER THAN A WOLFS — THEY ALSO SET OUTSIDE THE HEAD WIDTH.
YOU CAN EITHER LEAVE THE CARVING NATURAL OR PAINT IT!

COYOTE'S HEAD AND
LEFT FRONT PAW

HERE IS ANOTHER FAMILIAR POSE FOR THE COYOTE.
BE CREATIVE OR, MAYBE EVEN CARVE BOTH OF THESE BEAUTIES.

HAVE FUN AND KEEP CARVING!

TIGER
IN REPOSE

OVERSIZE
TO SHOW
DETAIL

PAD

BACK PAW

INSIDE

FRONT PAW

DETAIL OF
STRIPES

RIGHT SIDE

71

TIGER

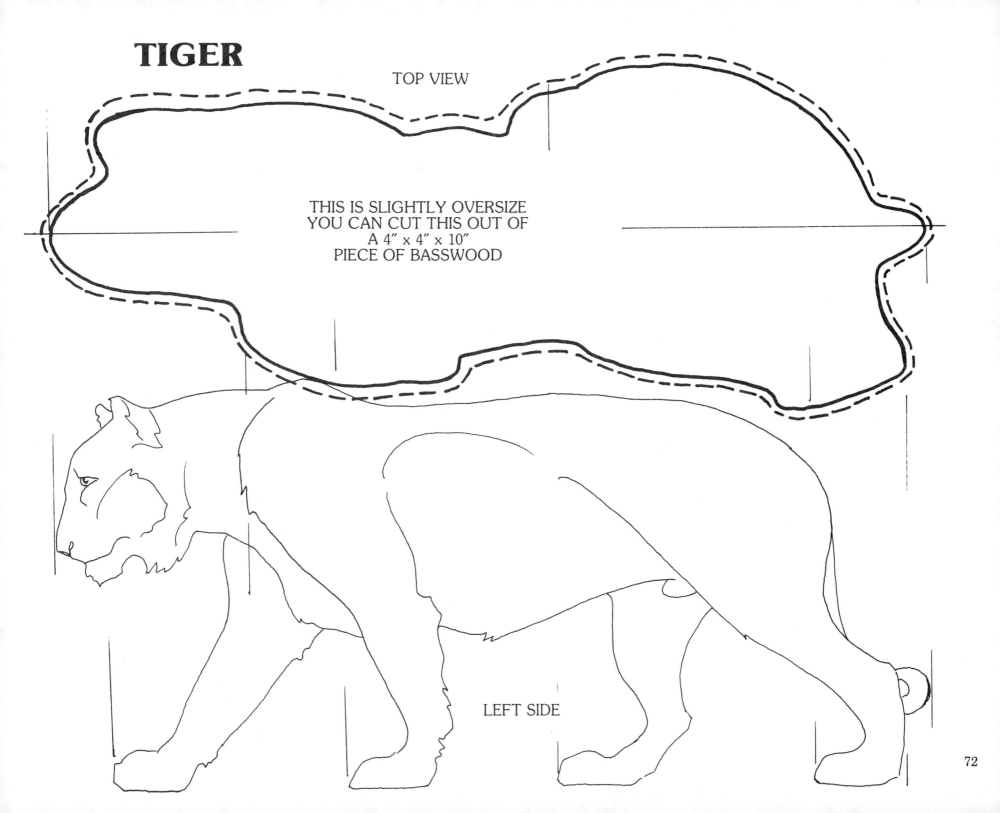

TOP VIEW

THIS IS SLIGHTLY OVERSIZE
YOU CAN CUT THIS OUT OF
A 4″ x 4″ x 10″
PIECE OF BASSWOOD

LEFT SIDE

72

"STOP AND SMELL THE FLOWERS"

THIS LITTLE RABBIT IS A FUN PROJECT
THAT CAN BE CARVED IN A FEW
HOURS — NOTE THE LINES TO
FOLLOW WHEN BURNING
THE HAIR TEXTURE.
KEEP YOUR LINES
SHARP AND CLEAN

SAW OVERSIZED

NOTE SHAPE
OF HEAD

RIGHT SIDE

CARVE THE HEAD FIRST!

TEXTURE THE FINISHED
CARVING WITH BURNING
IRON

LEFT SIDE

USE 1/16 ROD
TO MOUNT TO BASE

73

MOOSE

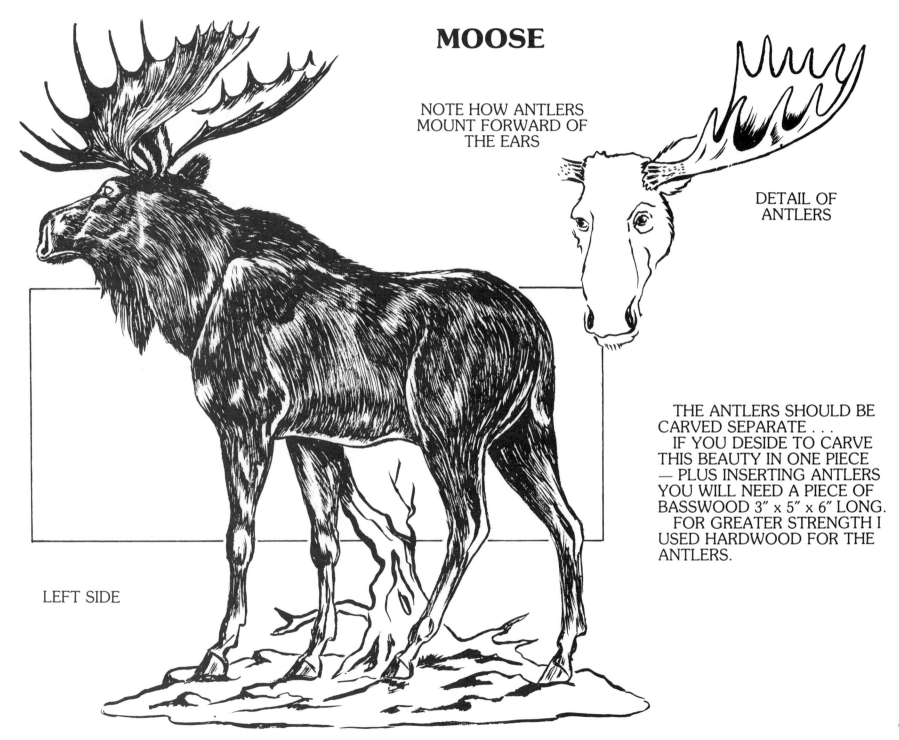

NOTE HOW ANTLERS
MOUNT FORWARD OF
THE EARS

DETAIL OF
ANTLERS

THE ANTLERS SHOULD BE
CARVED SEPARATE . . .
IF YOU DESIDE TO CARVE
THIS BEAUTY IN ONE PIECE
— PLUS INSERTING ANTLERS
YOU WILL NEED A PIECE OF
BASSWOOD 3" x 5" x 6" LONG.
FOR GREATER STRENGTH I
USED HARDWOOD FOR THE
ANTLERS.

LEFT SIDE

74

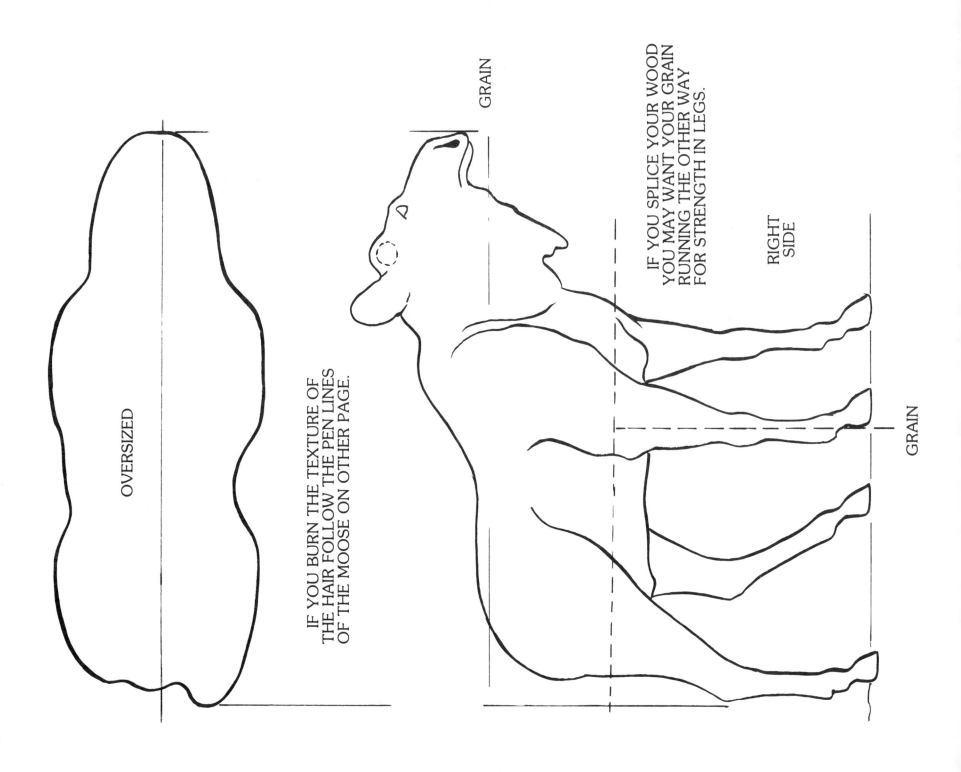

OVERSIZED

IF YOU BURN THE TEXTURE OF
THE HAIR FOLLOW THE PEN LINES
OF THE MOOSE ON OTHER PAGE.

GRAIN

IF YOU SPLICE YOUR WOOD
YOU MAY WANT YOUR GRAIN
RUNNING THE OTHER WAY
FOR STRENGTH IN LEGS.

RIGHT
SIDE

GRAIN

CHEETAH

THE FASTEST ANIMAL ON 4 LEGS
(to 70 mph) EXTREMELY LONG LEGS
GANGLY BODY, AND A SMALL
HEAD

DETAIL OF HEAD

CLAWS BLUNT
PARTLY RETRACTILE

DETAIL OF
RIGHT FRONT
PAW

TEXTURE
BODY WITH SHORT
FINE HAIR LINES

EYES
YELLOW

GRAIN

ANCHOR TO
BASE

LEFT SIDE

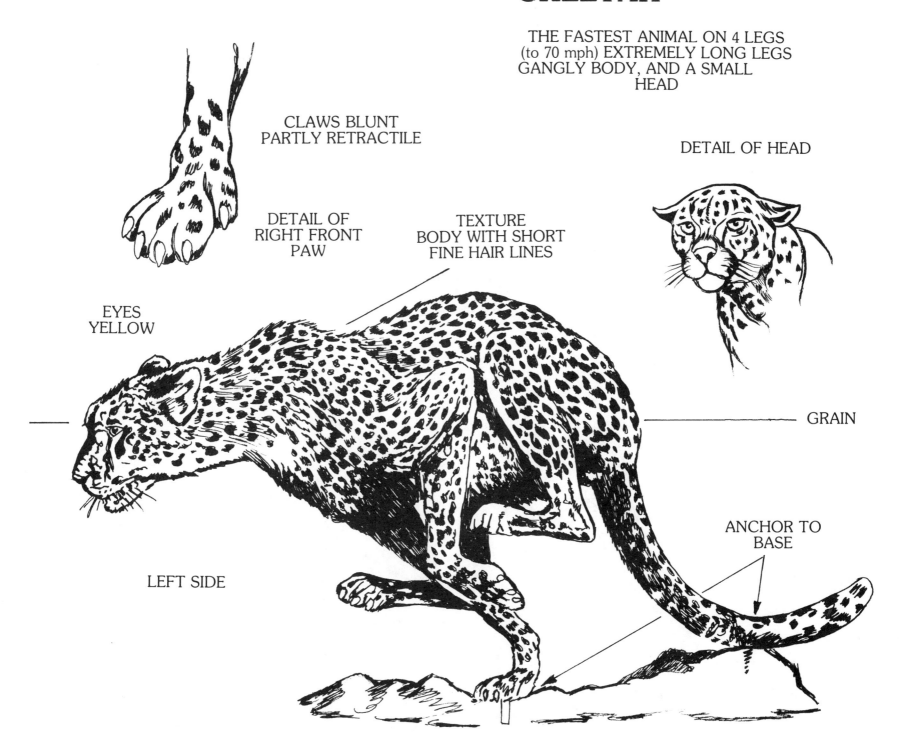

76

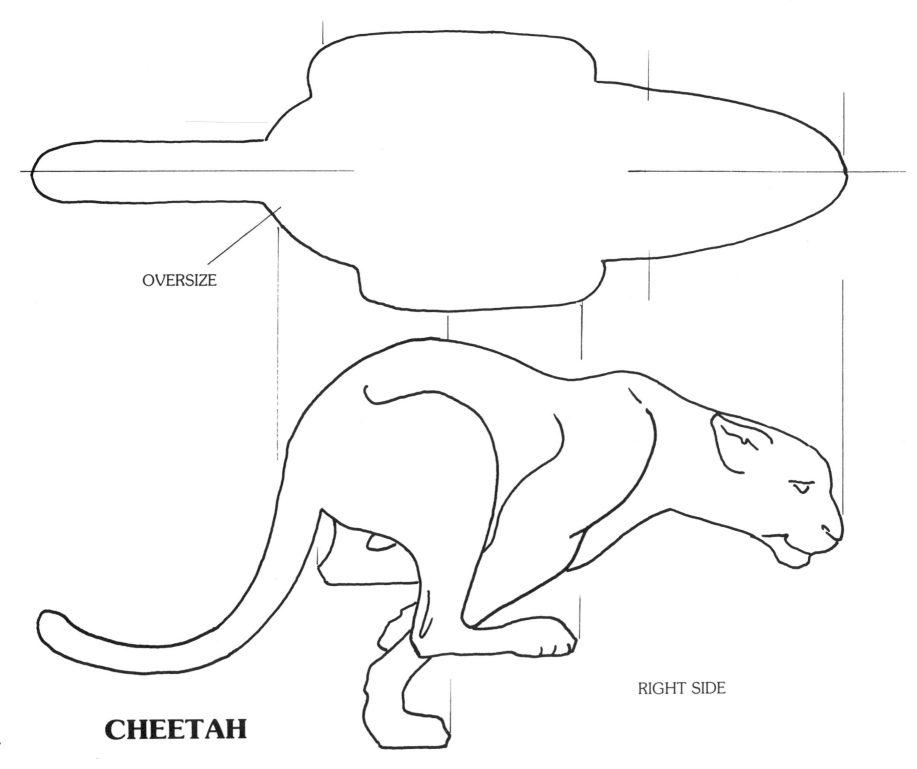

OVERSIZE

RIGHT SIDE

CHEETAH

77

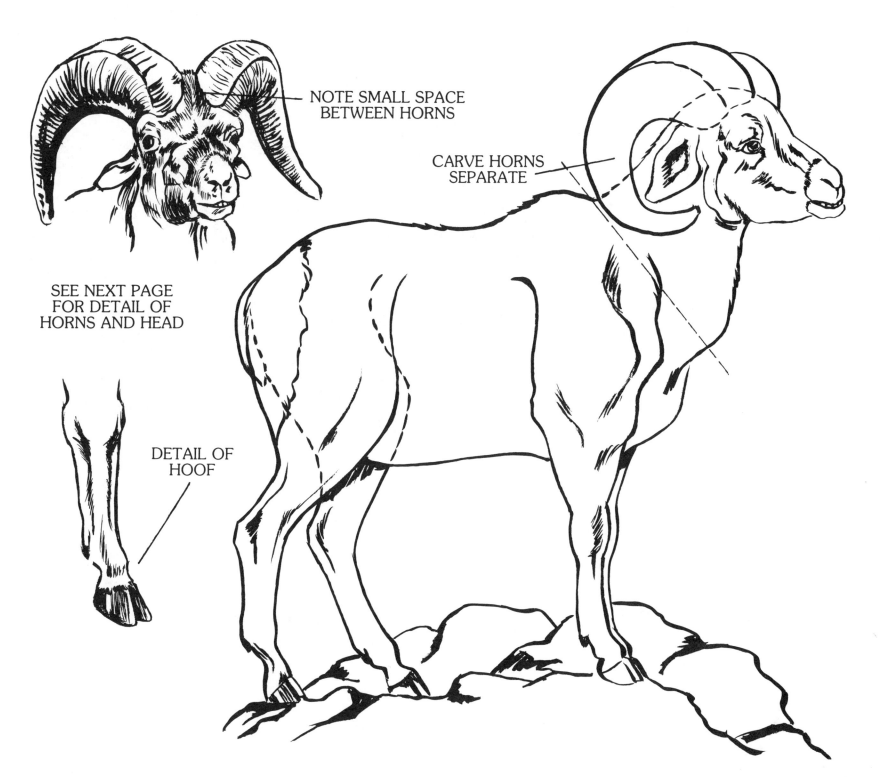

NOTE SMALL SPACE
BETWEEN HORNS

CARVE HORNS
SEPARATE

SEE NEXT PAGE
FOR DETAIL OF
HORNS AND HEAD

DETAIL OF
HOOF

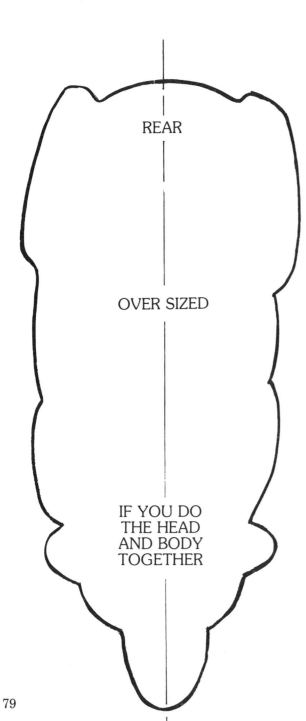

REAR

OVER SIZED

IF YOU DO
THE HEAD
AND BODY
TOGETHER

ROCKY MOUNTAIN
BIGHORN SHEEP

I WOULD SUGGEST THAT YOU CARVE THE HEAD AND
THE HORNS SEPARATE FROM THE BODY — IT WILL BE
EASIER TO CARVE THE HEAD AND EARS — THEN PUT ON
THE HORNS . . .

HOWEVER YOU DESIDE TO CARVE THIS BEAUTY . . . THE
HORNS WILL PROVE TO BE THE CHALLENGE . . . HAVE FUN,
AND SELECT A GOOD BASE FOR THIS FINE PIECE . . .

BELLE AND CACTUS PETE

MANY A MAN HAS BEEN PLANTED IN BOOTHILL BECAUSE OF LAUGHTER . . .

WHEN OLD CACTUS PETE AND DANCEHALL BELLE GO OUT FOR A MOONLIGHT STROLL IN THEIR FINEST ATTIRE NO ONE DARES TO EVEN SMILE. IF CACTUS DON'T GET YOU "BUTCH", BELLE'S VICIOUS DOG, WILL.

THESE TWO CHARACTERS WERE CARVED BECAUSE I HAD SOME NICE PIECES OF WOOD, THAT WERE TOO SMALL FOR A DUCK OR BIRD — REALLY I GOT A KICK OUT OF THIS CARVING.

CACTUS PETE

CARVE THE HEAD FIRST. TRY TO KEEP
THE REFINED, DIGNIFIED LOOK THAT I
HAVE GIVEN HIM . . .

WHEN YOU ATTACH THE
HEAD TO THE BODY BE
SURE IT SETS DOWN DEEP
ENOUGH. YOU MAY WANT
TO TURN THE HEAD
SLIGHTLY . . .
HE SHOULDN'T HAVE TOO
LONG A NECK.

YOU CAN CREATE YOUR
OWN DESIGN ON HIS VEST,
AND NECK PIECE.

NOTE SQUARE
TOE ON HIS
BOOTS

KEEP HEAD
LEVEL . . SO HE'S
LOOKING RIGHT AT YOU

DANCE HALL BELLE

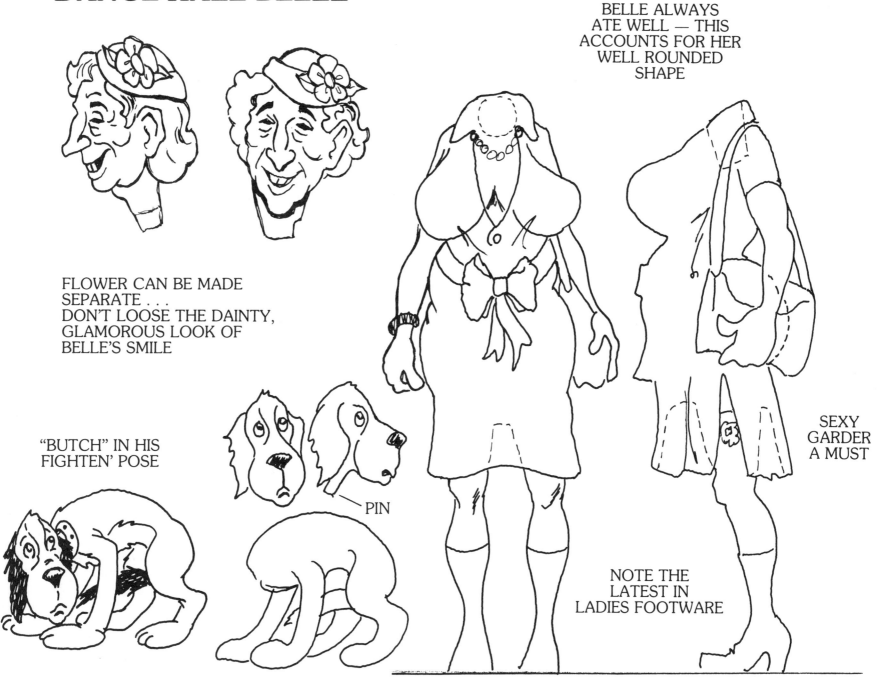

BELLE ALWAYS ATE WELL — THIS ACCOUNTS FOR HER WELL ROUNDED SHAPE

FLOWER CAN BE MADE SEPARATE . . . DON'T LOOSE THE DAINTY, GLAMOROUS LOOK OF BELLE'S SMILE

"BUTCH" IN HIS FIGHTEN' POSE

PIN

SEXY GARDER A MUST

NOTE THE LATEST IN LADIES FOOTWARE

INDEX

Index - continued

Suppliers   Listed   Geographically

ALABAMA

Craft Village/Chez La Roque	Rte. #3 , Box 148, Hwy #59S.	Foley	AL	36535

ARKANSAS

Arkansas Valley Woodcarvers	Box 1849	Russellville	AR	72801
Cabe Enterprise Inc.	Route 1, Box 176	Hattieville	AR	72063
Laughlin's Woodcarving Sply	Rte. 6 Box 147	Harrison	AR	72601

ARIZONA

Dave Rushlo Carvers Supply	2530 N. 80th Place	Scottsdale	AZ	85257

CALIFORNIA

Nemy Electric Tool Co.	7635 A Auburn Blvd.	Citrus Heights	CA	95610
The Wild Duck	9785 Live Oak Dr.	Ben Lomond	CA	95005
Wood N Stuff	650 Blue Oak Dr.	Ukiah	CA	95482
Wood Works	14007 Midland Rd.	Poway	CA	92064

CANADA

Al's Decoys Supplies	27 Connaught Ave.	London, Ontario	CN	N5Y 3A4
Bedrock Supply	9617 63rd Ave.	Edmonton, Alberta	CN	T6E 0G2
Burdette Gallery	R R # 2	Orton, Ontario	CN	LON INO
Canadian Woodworker	1391 St. James St.	Winnipeg	MB	R3H 0Z1
CAN-DO Bookstore	311 Queen St. West	Toronto, Ontario	CN	M5V 2A4
CORNERSTONE BOOKS	R.R. #2 , Box 250	Tavistock, Ontario	CN	NOB 2R0
Decoy Carving Supplies	59 Woodcrest Ave.	St. Albert, Alberta	CN	T8N 3H8
Exotic Woods	2483 Industrial St.	Burlington , Ontario	CN	L7P 1A6
Gene's Woodcarving&Supplies	116 West 27th St.	Hamilton, Ontario	CN	
Wild Bird Co.	760 Bedford Hwy.	Bedford	NS	B4A 1A2
Lee Valley Tools	1080 Morrison Dr.	Ottawa , Ontario	CN	K2H 8K7
Nautilus Arts and Crafts	6075 Kingston Rd.	West Hill , Ontario	CN	M1C 1K5
Primus Woodcrafting Supply	Box 658	Fort Langley, B.C.	CN	VOX 1J0
Wood N Feathers	R R # 3	Ashton, Ontario	CN	K0A 1B0
WoodChips Carving Supplies	3617 E. 4th Ave	Vancouver, British Columbia	CN	V5M 1M2
Welbeck Sawmill	RR#1	Durham , Ontario	CN	NOG 1R0

Wildlife Carvings	RR # 3	Brockville, Ontario	CN	K6V 5T3
Bird's Eye Nature Store	177 Queen St. S.	Charlotttetown, PEI	CN	C1A 4B4
McGray Wildlife Sculpture	RR # 2	Wiarton, Ontario	CN	NOH 2T0
House of Tools	Unit 9, 805 Circle Dr. E.	Saskatoon, Saskatchewan	CN	S7K 3S4
House of Tools	Bay 5, 2920- 32 Ave. NE	Calgary, Alberta	CN	T1Y 5J4
House of Tools	8228 MacLeod Trail SE	Calgary, Alberta	CN	T2M 2B8
House of Tools	100 Mayfield Common NW	Edmonton, Alberta	CN	T5P 4K9
House of Tools	8737 50th St.	Edmonton, Alberta	CN	T6B 1E7
Wood N Works	460 2nd Ave. N.	,Saskatoon, Saskatchewan	CN	S7K 2C3

COLORADO

Beaver Hut	11091 W. 44th Ave.	Wheatridge	CO	80033
Mountain Woodcarvers	Box 3485	Estes Park	CO	80517
Woodcraft Supply Corp.	4403 S. Tamarac Pkway	Denver	CO	

CONNECTICUT

Woodcarvers Shop	464 Pratt St.	Meriden	CT	06450

FLORIDA

Quality Carving Supplies	28 River Front Dr.	Venice,	FL	34293

GEORGIA

Woodworkers Choice	5290 S. ShoreDr.	Conyers	GA	30208

IOWA

Woodcraft Shop	2724 State St.	Bettendorf	IA	52722

IDAHO

Wood N' Things	601 E. 44th St. #3	Boise	ID	83714

ILLINOIS

Feather Craft Carving Inc.	61 Country Club Acres	Belleville	IL	62223
NSK America Corp.	2035 S. Arlington Hts. Rd. #112	Arlington Heights	IL	60005
Stuarts Woodcarvers Supply	RR#1	Kirkwood	IL	61447

INDIANA

Paul Mills Carving Supplies	513 East hawthorn St.	Fort Wayne	IN	46806
Woodcrafters Supply Center	3250 N. Post Rd. Suite 180	Indianapolis	IN	46226

KANSAS

Freeborns Woodcarving Splies	7909 W. 80 Terrace	Overland Park	KS	66204

KENTUCKY

Manny's Woodworker's Place	602 S. Broadway	Lexington	KY	40508

LOUISIANA

Curt's Waterfowl Corner	Box 228,123 LeBoeuf St.	Montegut	LA	70377

MASSACHUSETTS

Carvers Plus	141 West St.	Leominster	MA	01453
Hanson Carving Barn	201 High St.	Hanson	MA	02341
Woodcraft Supply Corp.	313 Montvale	Woburn	MA	01888

MARYLAND

CraftWoods	2101 Greenspring Drive	Timonium	MD	21093

MAINE

MDI Woodcarvers Supply	228 Main St.	Bar Harbor	ME	04609
Knock On Wood	Rte. #1	Baring	ME	04694

MICHIGAN

Frankenmuth WoodcarvingStudi	976 S. Main St.	Frankenmuth	MI	48734
Highwood Bookshop	Box 1246	Traverse City	MI	49684
Jerrys Decoy Supplies	9536 West Seven Mile Road	Northville	MI	48167
The Duck Blind	8721-B Gull Road	Richland	MI	49083
Troy Woodcraft	301 Scottsdale	Troy	MI	48084
Woodcraft Supply Corp.	14695 Telegraph Rd.	Redford	MI	

MINNESOTA

Ivan Whillock Studio	122 First Ave. N. E.	Faribault	MN	55021
Wood Gallery & Supplies	Holiday Mall Shopping Center	Moorehead	MN	56560
Woodcarvers Supply Co.	3056 Excelsior Blvd.	Minneapolis	MN	55416
Woodcraft Supply Corp.	9741 Lyndale Ave. S.	Bloomington	MN	
Jennings Decoy Co.	601 Franklin N.E.	St. Cloud	MN	56304

MISSOURI

Paxton Lumber Co.	6311 St. John Ave.	Kansas City	MO	64123
Woodcraft Supply Corp.	12511 Olive Blvd.	Creve Cour	MO	

MONTANA

North West Carving Supplies	Box 407	Manhattan	MT	59741

NEBRASKA

Midwest Woodworkers	13209 I St.	Omaha	NE	68137

NEW JERSEY

Books Plus	113 St. Joseph Blvd., Box 731	Lodi	NJ	07644
Colwood Electronics	One Meridian Rd.	Eatontown	NJ	07724
Wildife Carvings	114 Amber St.	Beach Haven	NJ	08008

NEW YORK

Buck Run Carving Supplies	781 Gully Road	Aurora	NY	13026
Constantine's	2050 Eastchester Rd.	Bronx	NY	10461
Frank Mittermeier, Inc.	3577 E. Temont Ave.	Bronx	NY	10465
Syracuse Woodcarving Supply	2612 Erie Blvd. East	Syracuse	NY	13224
Warren Tool Co. Inc.	2209- Route 9 G	Rhinebeck	NY	12572
Garrett Wade Mailorder	161 Avenue of the Americas	New York	NY	10013

OHIO

Forest Products	Box 12	Avon	OH	44011
Han D Crafts	33 Watervliet Ave.	Dayton	OH	45420
Woodcarvers Cove	4995 Telegraph Road. Rte. #113	So. Amherst	OH	44001
Woodcrafters Supply Co.	5331 Sinclair Rd.	Columbus	OH	
Woodworkers' Store	2500 East Main St.	Columbus	OH	43209

OREGON

Woodcrafters Lumber Sales Inc.	212 N.E. Sixth	Portland	OR	97232

PENNSYLVANIA

Elmer Jumper	142 DiMarco Dr.	Philadelphia	PA	19154
Grizzly Tool Imports East	2406 Reach Rd.	Williamsport	PA	17701
J.H. Kline Carving Shop	Box 445, Forge Hill Rd.	Manchester	PA	17345
Ritter Carvers Inc.	1559 Dillon Road	Maple Glen	PA	19002
Susquehanna Decoy Shop	Kitchen Kettle Village	Intercourse	PA	17534
Wood Cut N Stuff	RR# 4 , Box 4304	Berwick	PA	18603
Woodworkers World	1509 Lititz Pike	Lancaster	PA	17601

SOUTH DAKOTA

Van Dyke's	catalog department	Woonsocket	SD	57385

TENNESSEE

Smoky Mountain Woodcarvers	Box 103	Louisville	TN	37777

TEXAS

Knotty But Nice Woodcarving	1112 South Hampton Rd.	Angleton	TX	77515
Tool Box-Richard Spinney	6065 Townhouse Lane.	Beaumont	TX	77701
Williams Tool Co.	2017 White Settlement Rd.	Fort Worth	TX	76107
Lone Star Carving Supply	2309 Brookdale	Garland	TX	75040

VIRGINIA

Chesapeake Bay Woodcrafters	4307 Hanover Ave.	Richmond	VA	23221
Little Mountain Carving	Rte. #2, Box 1329	Front Royal	VA	22630
Mountain Heritage Crafters	601 Quail Dr.	Bluefield	VA	24605
P.C. English	6201 Mallard Rd. Box 380	Thornburg	VA	22565
Woodcarvers Supply Inc.	Box 8928	Norfolk	VA	23503

catalog house - mail order only

WASHINGTON

Cascade Carvers Supply	198 Galaxie Road	Chehalis	WA	98532
Grizzly Tool Imports West	Box 2069	Bellingham	WA	98227
Woodcraft Supply Corp.	5963 Corson Ave. S.	Seattle	WA	

WISCONSIN

Hunting Rig Books 453 Pendleton Rd. Neenah, WI 54956

WEST VIRGINIA

Woodcraft Supply Corp. 201 Wood County Industrial Pk Parkersburg WV 26102-1686

Suppliers names and addresses listed above and elsewhere in this book are provided as a service to the woodcarving hobby only. Appearance in this book is not to be considered a recommendation or endorsement of any kind.

PUBLICATIONS / CLUBS / SHOWS

"One of our greatest assets is the carving clubs that have developed all over the country. If you don't belong - join. The members are so friendly, and always willing to help with questions you may have."

GEORGE LEHMAN

Originally, we had planned to include a listing of all the woodcarving clubs and shows across North America similar to the above section on suppliers. Unfortunately, the size and organization of these makes this unfeasible at this time. If you are a member of a club, please send the club name and address to us here at **FOX CHAPEL PUBLISHING, BOX 7948X, LANCASTER, PA 17604-7948** and we will try to include these in the next edition. What we recommend to stay in touch with what's happening are the following publications:

CHIP CHATS
Published by the National Woodcarvers Association   This must be one of the greatest values for the woodcarving hobbyist. A slick color filled magazine plus membership for only $10.00 per year. A real must. (see address in following pages.)

WILDFOWL CARVING AND COLLECTING
Box 1831
Harrisburg, PA 17105   Fact and color filled magazine. Very comprehensive show listings.

WILDFOWL ART- Journal of the Ward Foundation
1819 Bay Ridge Avenue
Annapolis MD 21403   Quality magazine put out by this pioneering organization.

BIRDERS' WORLD
720 East 8th St.
Holland MI 49423   Not a carving magazine exactly but packed with photos that would be useful references for carvers.

FINALLY!

A magazine just for you, the bird carving enthusiast!

Written exclusively for bird carvers and collectors, Wildfowl Carving & Collecting is the perfect combination of inspiration, instruction and recreation.

Learn from the Masters
Discover New Carving and Painting Techniques
Enjoy Every Facet of this Uniquely American Art Form

- Rich, full color photos of masterpiece carvings
- Start-to-finish carving and painting projects
- Live-bird reference photos
- Complete listing of competitions and exhibits nationwide

Don't wait any longer! Complete the form to the right and start your subscription today!

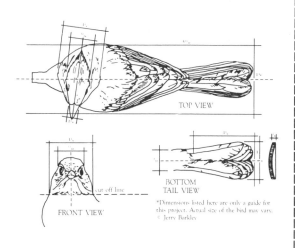

TOP VIEW

FRONT VIEW

BOTTOM TAIL VIEW

*Dimensions listed here are only a guide for this project. Actual size of the bird may vary.
© Jerry Barkley

JOIN THE WARD FOUNDATION / MUSEUM

DEDICATED TO PRESERVE, PROMOTE, PERPETUATE *Wildfowl Art*

WILDFOWL ART MUSEUM
WILDFOWL ART JOURNAL
EDUCATIONAL SEMINARS & WORKSHOPS

WARD WORLD CARVING COMPETITION
ART EXHIBITION & SALE
MEMBERSHIP SERVICES

CALL 1-800-742-4988

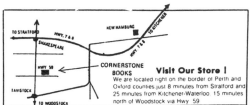